*A Series of Dogs*

# A Series of Dogs

JOHN ARMSTRONG

Dogs
Dogs
Dogs
Dogs
Dogs
Dogs
Dogs
Dogs

 NEW STAR BOOKS · VANCOUVER · 2016

NEW STAR BOOKS LTD.
newstarbooks.com • info@newstarbooks.com

#107–3477 Commercial St    1574 Gulf Road, #1517
Vancouver, BC              Point Roberts, WA
V5N 4E8 CANADA             98281 USA

The publisher acknowledges the financial support of the Canada Council for the Arts, the Government of Canada through the Canada Book Fund, the British Columbia Arts Council, and the Province of British Columbia through the Book Publishing Tax Credit.

Cataloguing information for this book is available from Library and Archives Canada, collectionscanada.gc.ca

Printed & bound in Canada on 100% post-consumer recycled paper by Imprimerie Gauvin, Gatineau, QC

ISBN 978-1-55420-118-1
Cover design by Oliver McPartlin
Typeset by New Star Books
First printing, November 2016

For Lynda, whose idea it was, and for Penny, who saw it through, and for John Lekich, who fixed it when I couldn't.

*Author's Note*

Despite this book's title, alert readers will discover the occasional cat has found its way into these pages. Do not complain to your bookseller: this wasn't the author's intention but he's learned over the course of years that cats do as they please and there's no keeping one out if he really wants in. Anyway, he'll just want back out in a minute. Accordingly, there will be no refunds.

*Chapter One*

# Ruff

*Life is a series of dogs.*

—GEORGE CARLIN

It's generally accepted that the place to begin is at the beginning, and in the beginning, my mother and I lived with my grandmother, my Uncle John, my Aunt Roberta (called Bobbie) and a dog named Ruff on a farm outside of Extension Ridge, near the Chase River on Vancouver Island. It was an isolated place with the nearest neighbour some miles down the road and when I look it up now Extension doesn't even rate the dignity of "town" or village"; it's listed in the government maps as an "area," defined as "a tract of land without homogeneous character or boundaries."

From my perspective it had plenty of character—I had my own cow, Bossie, and got my milk from her daily, so I'm told. When I was older I rode her as often as she allowed. By ride, I mean that I enticed her to the fence with grass and then climbed aboard, where she ignored me and clomped along at her regular cow-speed, going nowhere in particular and, often, no-where at all. One end of the pasture was much like the other and Bossie had seen it all anyway. As cows go, you could say that she was jaded.

I have no idea how we ended up with Ruff, who in the only picture I have of him is a very large Shepherd-cross with an enormous black head and a correspondingly large dog-smile, black lips drawn back from rows of pyramid-shaped teeth bared happily as he sits beside my highchair. It does not diminish his affection for me to note that I was a notoriously clumsy eater as a child, and that Ruff has positioned himself to catch whatever I drop. This is likely the beginning of my lifelong practice of feeding dogs at the table. The dogs like it, I like it, and as far as I am concerned, the rest of the world is simply misguided.

He started off as my Uncle John's dog but family mythology holds that once I arrived Ruff adopted me and appointed himself my bodyguard. This may be true: I honestly have no true recollection of him, ex-cept for disjointed fragments of sound and taste and touch, and something warm and dog-smelling in the haze of early memory, inextricably linked to the smell of the oil stove in the kitchen and wet shoes.

When I picture that farmhouse in my mind it's in black and white, and so are the inhabitants, because the only memories I really have of it are tied to a paper bag full of Kodak snapshots. Over the years our family stories and those photos have merged together in my mind until I have no way of unravelling what

I remember for myself and what my mind has spun together from these fragments. Like most histories, then, this is the agreed upon version of events from eyewitnesses, who are notoriously unreliable, and we're stuck with it.

My grandmother was a Prairie pioneer woman who I can't recall ever laughing, likely because she had little to laugh about. She had eight children who survived, and lived through at least three wars her men fought in. She brushed her teeth with ashes from the fireplace until she was past fifty and for the rest of her life was embarrassed by the extravagance of buying toothpaste. She went bankrupt numerous times as the family farmed and failed its way west and was an old woman by the time I was born.

Grandma did not hold with dogs in the house. Dogs, to her mind, were there to run off tramps and fight any wild animal that came into the yard. Ruff strongly favoured dogs being inside and there they met, on either side of the threshold.

Despite his size Ruff was adept at somehow oozing bonelessly into the kitchen from the back porch where his food and water dishes were kept. He would slip through the legs of anyone who went out the door and materialize between my high chair and the stove, until my grandmother discovered him and banished him again. It was a game they played endlessly and without any possibility of either winning. Eventually they became exhausted by it and agreed to simply pretend the other didn't exist, so long as Ruff didn't bark indoors.

My grandmother, my mother claimed, even began to stir some bacon drippings into his food and then walk past him, completely disregarding the dog-who-wasn't-there, in order to put his dish outside and call him. Ruff would follow her out the door and then come around the side of her legs to accept the bowl and wag thanks, both of them acting surprised to see the other, such was their dedication to preserving the *détente*.

The most famous story about Ruff is the time he held Auntie Mae hostage for the better part of a day. This was told so many times that it became a set-piece, polished and honed by repetition and as much a part of Christmas dinner or any family get-together as turkey or presents.

Uncle John was out working somewhere with a packed lunch, which meant he would not be back until near dark; a farmer's hours were "from can't-see to can't-see," and started at, as Grandma called it, "sparrow-chirp." Auntie Bobbie was working in the town of Nanaimo and would not be back before dinner.

My mother and Grandma were going to town to shop and run errands, and likely stop at the restaurant where the lady would read their tea leaves. Rather than them hauling me around all day Auntie Mae had volunteered to babysit. My Uncle Mac dropped her off at the gate and went off on his own for a day of fishing and drinking. Depending on the variables of that equation, he might be gone for days.

Seeing Mae down at the end of the drive, several

hundred yards of gravel and hard-pack dirt, Mom and Grandma waved to her and set me in my Jolly Jumper—a sort of bungee-type affair that could be strung up in doorways—and started down to meet her, mindful of not missing their bus, which ran only once or twice a day each way.

There were quick pecks and hugs as they passed and Mom and Grandma hustled the last bit as the bus driver, seeing them wave, slowed down. Then they were gone and Mae was climbing the front stairs, a little dusty and thirsty. I gurgled and drooled and bounced in happiness, and Mae came for me gurgling back and smiling. At which point Ruff rose up from where he was lying beside my jumper and growled low in his throat, head down and shoulders hunched, hackles up.

This stopped Mae in her tracks, and who would blame her? She was halfway across the porch, the stairs a few feet behind her, the front door and my own precious self directly ahead, and a large dog between us.

Ruff lay down but kept his eyes pinned on her. She took a step forward and he growled deeply. She stepped back and he stopped. She took a step further back, towards the stairs—thinking she could go around the house and get in through the back—and he half rose, growling again. That narrowed the options somewhat.

Mae was a small and somewhat round lady but she was game, and she sidled nonchalantly towards the side of the porch, thinking to climb over the rail and get down to the ground again. But Ruff was having none of that, either.

So there we stayed. Ruff would allow Mae to sit where she was, on the floorboards of the porch, but not to move more than a few inches in any direction. I was no help at all, and bounced and babbled in my jumper and then slept for the remainder of Mae's house arrest. She ran out of cigarettes in the first hour—she had only rolled enough for the trip to our house. She got more than a little thirsty and at the same time, desperately needed to pee.

It was a hot, dry summer day, where you can smell the dirt of the road and the softening tar, and there was little to do on that porch but sit listening to the grasshoppers jumping in the yard and the occasional car coming down the road and fading away again.

Over the years Aunt Mae's time on that porch grew in the telling and re-telling of the story, but it was surely several hours at least, and an hour with a full bladder is considerably longer than one with a bathroom handy.

Sometime later Mom and Grandma returned and Ruff ran down the stairs to meet them while Mae ran inside. When she came out Ruff was completely civil to her and gave no indication he had ever had any doubts about her at all. She was cool towards him from that point on, though Ruff never held a grudge over what he had already dismissed as a regrettable misunderstanding.

That's all I really know about Ruff. He was gone by

the time I was walking and talking. I asked my mother what happened to him and she said, "He ate fish and ran wild with the Indian dogs."

That was like saying "stolen by Gypsies." The Indian dogs never went inside a house except to steal, killed chickens and ate the henhouse eggs whenever they could, and otherwise took what they could find, fought and played and howled in the moonlight, and ran as a pack through the trees and across the fields. My family thought this was shameful but I could see the attraction. It sounded like a pretty good deal to me, even as a kid.

The "ate fish" part was a critical element of Ruff's downfall. Dogs who ate fish off the riverbank went wild—this was a deeply held truth in my family. It was shorthand for rejecting the laws of God and man, but it was also magical. It was understood that wild fish contained some element that produced a change like Dr. Jekyll's potion, reverting animals who ate of it to their savage, primal state: "nature, red in tooth and claw," as my Grandma put it, believing she was quoting the Bible. (I did, too until I looked it up years later and found it was Lord Tennyson, though one Lord is as good as another, I imagine.)

My family held a number of beliefs like this, and where they came from, who knew? Some years later I drove Auntie Mae to the doctor's office. She was suffering from cramps, nausea, and cold sweats, and believed a pork roast had been the culprit. On the way home when I asked her what the diagnosis was, she said the doctor had agreed with her. Further, he had warned her that every side of pork contains a bit, no bigger than a dime, that is poison to humans, but that it cannot be identified by sight or smell and so when eating chops, cutlets, roast, bacon, ham, sausage or ribs, you were playing roulette. Sometimes you won, sometimes you lost.

In the nearly forty years since that conversation I have looked in vain to find any substantiation for that frightening piece of information. I can only imagine what he actually said and what Mae heard, which were surely two very different things. No one in my family had much education past the early grades, having been hauled out of class any time the farm needed them, which was often (though my Uncle John had the kind of bizarre amalgamation of unlikely fact one accumulates from a meandering education through the public library and serious devotion to the daily crossword puzzle.)

It could be that the doctor had lectured her on the dangers of food poisoning and that leaving a pork roast out on the sideboard too long before cooking, rather than keeping it in the fridge, could be dangerous. He may have said that even a tiny piece of spoiled meat—say, the size of a dime—could cause serious illness. Knowing we were farm people and ate locally butchered meat he may have cautioned how easily fresh pork spoils, and any mention of bacteria or microbes would have been sufficient to cause terror.

At any rate, Mae heard what she heard, edited and

augmented it internally, and boiled it down to a new medical fact: all pork contains a deadly hidden poison, caused by invisible scientific microbes.

Not that this stopped her, or the other women in the family, from cooking pork regularly. I can still see her eyeing the pork chops on her plate with suspicion, approaching them with knife and fork held at an awkward distance from her body, as if she were about to snip the wires on a ticking bomb.

Nor did it stop her or anyone else in the family from feeding pork scraps to Ruff and other, later dogs; another belief in our family was that dogs had some magical ability to know what was safe to eat and what wasn't. The fact that dogs regularly died from eating poisoned food set out for rats was one of those inconvenient facts that was simply never discussed by unspoken agreement. No one in my family ever changed a belief once they had adopted it. Such behaviour was known to lead to atheism and other, even worse practices.

After Ruff, I don't recall any other dogs on the farm that were strictly ours. There were neighbour dogs that came visiting—one was a black and grey border collie and what-have-you cross that loved to chase the cows. I was often sent out to run him away from the pasture but when it was discovered I spent more time helping him terrorize the herd than I did defending them, I lost the job. Grandma took it over, stomping through them after the instigator of the uproar, waving a stick of kindling and shouting threats. I don't think it calmed any of the cows, particularly—there was a dog snapping and barking at their ankles on one side of them and a crazy old lady in a dress and gumboots on the other, yelling and waving a club. Between the two of them it's surprising the cows didn't give butter instead of milk.

After Ruff ran wild I can't remember ever seeing him again, though I have a vague, dreamlike picture of him across a field and me calling him, and him looking at me for a long moment before turning to run back into the woods with his pack. But it's not a trustworthy memory. It has the whiff of a movie scene, so distorted and dimly remembered that it's taken root as something that actually happened.

Whether it did or not, the outcome stays the same. He was gone and I was dogless for a very long time.

*Chapter Two*

# The Dingo and Kiltie

When I was about ten or eleven we moved back to the Lower Mainland. My mother gave living with my father another try and after that failed we lived in a variety of low-rent apartments in Vancouver. The place we stayed longest was the Little Mountain Housing Project, a government low-income sprawl of two-storey, four-apartment buildings, five or so blocks square and cut up into crisscrossing pathways with idyllic names like Bluejay Lane and Primrose Court—though there were no primroses to be seen and too much concrete and blacktop for a blue jay to find much of interest in.

The place was filled to capacity with single mothers on assistance and all of us desperate to get out. It was a sad little community; the only laughter was the sound of older kids torturing the younger ones on the tarmac "playgrounds" set out behind each group of buildings, and the shrieking sounds of their mothers, leaning off the back porches and stairs that covered the rear of each apartment block, like some hellish trellis twined with loud, angry flowers.

My mother was no less eager to escape than the rest of them. She met a Scot at a Legion dance, an ex-airman named Arthur who bore an unsettling resemblance to Bela Lugosi. Arthur held some dreadful jobs, graveyard shifts servicing fluorescent light fixtures from a rickety ladder high above deserted factory floors, or working twelve-hour shifts managing a car park rotating back and forth between five a.m. and five p.m. starts. All of them were seen as steps toward a single goal: one day we would escape into an actual house, and in their wildest moments he and my mother even dreamed of someday getting the down payment together to buy one.

This is why he took a second job caretaking a pair of side-by-side apartment buildings shortly after we began living with him. The job came with a two-bedroom suite included as part of the wages, and with my mother doing the actual caretaking, we were able to save money, inching ever closer to the dream. I didn't much care about the dream—but if it meant I could finally have a dog then I was all for it.

The apartments we took over were the sort of two-storey stucco and wood trim buildings that had rows of tarnished brass mailboxes in the foyer and a plate glass foyer window with the name of the apartment in gilt script above the address numbers. The names bore no relation to anything at all, as if the developer had opened an encyclopedia at random, the way high school rock bands choose a name for their group, resulting in The Mozambique, which looked a little foolish under a foot of snow, or The Ambassador, which led you to ponder which impoverished nation would set their dignitary up in a studio apartment with parking on the street, though he would have Cablevision. The sign on the lawn said so.

Ours were named The Hollyhock and, in a bold and unexpected move away from the floral, The Gaylord. The day we moved in, my mother orchestrating the movers as they humped boxes up the walk, a man came out the front with a dog on a leash and held the glass door for us. My mother went through it still directing traffic but the sight stopped me in my tracks.

I don't know what kind of dog it was; my memory serves up an amorphous collection of fur, lolling tongue and black eyes, and it didn't matter. A dog is a dog is a dog and everything else is details. It was clear that one lived here, and if the owners allowed one, they had to allow another. Apparently I wouldn't have to wait until we could get a house after all.

I began my campaign immediately and my mother made the worst mistake she could have; she said, "We'll see." To a nine or ten-year-old, "No" means "Yes, but not right away" and "We'll see" means "Yes, my darling child, almost immediately."

My first day at the new school I went to the library and took out books on various dog breeds. Ideally, I was looking for one at least as big as my old cow Bossy, or perhaps a Clydesdale horse, and also ideally part wolf; something along the lines of Fenris, the giant wolf in the *Mighty Thor* comic books, by way of Jack London's

Buck. He would love me as a brother, and I him, but underneath it he would still be a red-eyed dealer of death from the primordial forest and if anyone tried to take my lunch or scatter my library books he would rip out their throats and we would run and laugh through fields of tall grass, or at least through the vacant lots on Broadway down past the funeral home near Oak Street.

I had narrowed it down to a Rottweiler, the dog who marched with the Roman legions and was famous for his bravery and loyalty, a mastiff, or possibly a giant Irish wolfhound. I was also greatly taken with Cerberus, the gatekeeper to Hades, but mythological three-headed puppies were in short supply.

I was treading as softly as I could bear to, only mentioning the fact we were still dogless as often as I thought necessary to keep the subject fresh and to make sure my restraint on the subject was not mistaken for indifference. I only broached it roughly every time I saw my mother, but just in passing, without badgering her about it. Just a reminder, still no dog here, in case it slipped your mind.

Weeks passed and then became months. All my research had gone out the window. I was bitterly disappointed but not discouraged. I'd waited this long—I could hold out a while more, but the pressure was building inside me. Everywhere I turned there were smiling furry faces and wagging tails, and joyous barking. The world was filled with dogs, and none of them mine. Dogs appeared in the schoolyard out of thin air, escapees from leash and fence and were fawned and fussed over for a recess or lunch period and then disappeared again. It was almost more than a boy could bear, and I finally cracked.

It happened while walking home from the bus stop on Oak Street and it hit me like the light hit Saul on the road to Damascus. The thunderbolt, the Sicilians call it—overwhelming love at first sight, obliterating everything else. The stomach falls through your feet like an astronaut in orbit, the world drops away in a blur of colour and muffled sound, reducing vision like the pinpoint of a surgical laser focused on the object of adoration: a dingo puppy in the window of the Fin & Feathers pet store on the south side of Broadway, a store I had been in many times but rarely even looked at now. It had mostly goldfish, small lizards and tropical birds though it carried the occasional tarantula, which was always noteworthy even if five minutes of tapping on the glass and staring at it meant twenty minutes of searching the bed and shaking the covers and curtains before crawling in at bedtime.

I knew it was a dingo because the sign behind the glass in the corner of his showcase pen said "Australian Dingo Puppy—$100." He was orangey-brown and white and roly-poly and when I stopped in front of the glass he went wild from the attention, scratching and climbing up the window trying to get through.

I stood there for a few minutes touching the glass and watching him before I realized all I had to do was go inside and I did, banging the door off the inside wall and setting the cockatiels and parrots and budgerigars to terrified squawking. The hamsters took it in stride but the man behind the counter leaped up and shouted at me. I had no time for him. My hands were already in the window box. The dingo was quivering with happiness and turning frantic circles of joy, wanting to be petted everywhere at once and I tried to oblige. He nipped and licked my hands with slobbery dog kisses. He was very lonely.

Is there any other animal that is instinctively happy to see a human being? A puppy will head straight to your hands even though it's never seen a human in its short little life. Even a stray mutt on the street who's been starved and beaten and abandoned will look at you with hope and anticipation, his innate attraction to humans inextinguishable. Dogs have a naturally high opinion of people that nothing we've done accounts for; they expect and anticipate the best from us and nothing will really dissuade them of it. Not even experience.

The pet store man got over his annoyance quickly. He could smell a sale coming. He had a love-struck boy in his store and all he had to do was put up with me until closing time and I'd be back, dragging a parent behind me. I'd do most of the work for him.

He answered questions until nearly five o'clock. As he locked the door behind us I begged him not to sell the pup until I could come back. He said, sadly, he couldn't guarantee anything. A lot of people were interested in this dog and he had to sell it to the first one who put money on the counter. It was a cold fact of business, he told me, turning the key in the lock. He wished things were otherwise but there it was.

This meant I had to move fast. A dog like this would surely be gone seconds after he opened in the morning. It seemed only blind luck he was still there at all. I ran home, rehearsing my argument all the way.

It did not begin well. I was late coming home from school and my mother was almost to the point of phoning the hospital emergency wards. There's a psychological syndrome called "catastrophic thinking" and if my family didn't pioneer it, they perfected it. This affliction is, simply, envisioning the worst possible outcome to any mundane situation, and then becoming as emotionally worked up as if it's actually happened.

One famous instance was the afternoon my mother phoned hers, my grandmother, several times over an hour or so and got no answer. She might have been asleep and not heard the phone, or in the bath, or walking around the block. But where's the fun in that when you can picture her comatose and bleeding on the kitchen floor, beside the can of peaches that fell from the shelf and laid her low? Or twisted and broken in agony at the bottom of the basement stairs, moaning for rescue? The longer my mother dwelled on it, the worse her imaginings became until she was near hysterical and insisted Arthur drive across town to check on her, even if only to cover the body with a blanket in respectful fashion. We piled into the little blue

Datsun and raced across town, running yellow lights and taking corners with a squeal of rubber. Whatever faults he had, and they were more than several, Arthur certainly entered into the spirit of neurotic imaginings wholeheartedly.

We turned onto her street on two wheels, stopping with a lurch in front of Grandma's and there she was, pulling weeds at the side of the house. My mother scrabbled from the car, weeping and thanking god in broken fragments of speech between gasps for air and great sobs of joy. Grandma got up off her knees, listened to it for a minute, shook her head and went inside to put the kettle on. She'd lived through multiple bankruptcies and wars, polio and influenza epidemics and the digging of graves for her children. She had no interest in manufacturing disasters. She'd had enough real ones.

My mother hadn't gotten herself anywhere near that state yet, though. "Phoning the hospitals" was one of the preliminary stages of hysteria, like the amber stage of the Terrorist Alert system. I don't recall my mother ever actually phoning a hospital, or the police for that matter, which was one rung up the ladder of mounting anxiety. By the time she was worked up enough to do so, it seemed pointless. At that point she had you beheaded, dismembered, and stuffed into a Hefty bag and all she really wanted was for them to find the remains, so they could be given Christian burial. The worst thing, she always said when the TV news reported on a missing child, would be not knowing . . .

This was not the ideal moment for broaching the subject of the dog. I knew I had to let the visions of bleached bones and shallow graves melt away, though I also knew that then I would really be in trouble. When you're missing, parents weep and tear their clothes with grief. They'd give anything to see your shining face just one more time. However, when you do turn up, they want to kill you. You just have to ride it out. I put an appropriately contrite expression on my face and rehearsed my sales pitch while they screamed at me.

Somewhere between the pork cutlets and creamed corn and the after-dinner tea, I sensed the moment and made my move. "I found the dog I want," I said casually, sliding it into the conversation almost unnoticed, like a cat through a picket fence. The idea was to skilfully introduce the subject into whatever Arthur and Mom were talking about and manoeuvre things so that one of them consented to the idea without actually recognizing what the topic was. It was a bold and elegant plan, and it failed completely.

"Dog? We're not getting any dog," Arthur said. He'd played his ace straight out of the gate and left me with only one card of my own to play. A ploy known in all families, and one guaranteed to raise voices, slam doors and leave someone crying.

"You said . . ." I countered. And we were off. He hadn't, he said, and I gave him the day and date, completely off the top of my head. Of course he had said no such thing but my entire argument rested on unshake-

20

able certainty, kin to the First Rule of Lying: know your story and stick to it no matter what.

The Second Rule is that you must believe completely in your story; I was ten or eleven years old and I could believe wholeheartedly in anything I put my mind to, and I could already see the clouds of doubt forming in Arthur's mind. He would never have said yes to a dog but could I have caught him at a weak moment, when he was distracted by bills or some household crisis? While he was watching TV? That was just my style, hitting him with something like that at a critical moment in one of his shows, when Mannix was trapped in a burning car or the wheels had come off Ironsides' wheelchair.

Then he sealed his own fate: "I meant we could have one someday, but not now. Not in an apartment."

My mother came to my rescue. "Mr. Gidding has a dog, in three ten."

Arthur couldn't believe she'd betrayed him. He had the look of a man reaching for his wallet and finding it no longer there, a dozen possibilities flashing through his mind and each rejected, leaving only the knowledge that yes, the universe and all its agents had conspired against him and he was screwed beyond all hope.

I had one hurdle left to jump. The dog cost a hundred dollars, but I had a difficult time conceiving exactly how much that really was. My allowance was two dollars a week and my frame of reference for all financial questions was the spinner rack at the drugstore, where a regular comic book was twelve cents, or eight to the dollar. I could see that my dingo was worth eight hundred comics plus the residual four cents on each dollar, which further computation showed to be ... more than I could do in my head and more than I could spring on the adults at one sitting. Arthur was still stirring his tea in silent fury, clanging the spoon against the sides of the cup like a little fire bell. Best to leave it alone for now. Still, I was halfway home, or rather, the dingo was. If I could show how to get the dog without the adults going into their pockets, the job was done.

In this, I had unconsciously hit on the First Rule of Selling, reiterated to me years later when I worked, briefly, at a Murray Goldman's menswear store. "Remove the objections," the old salesman advised me—Murray was maybe fifty but seemed decades older. He wore a tape measure around his neck and looked as if he would have a hard time bending over far enough to tie his shoes but he could whip that tape into action and be down there measuring an inseam with alarming speed. His belief was that the customer rarely knew what they wanted or if they did, they were wrong. He, on the other hand, knew precisely what they needed and by happy coincidence, happened to have the very item in stock. Whether they wanted it or liked it made no difference—they were going home with it if he had his way, with a little luck maybe even wearing it out of the store. If it was too long, he told them to stand up straight. It it was too large, it was "a nice comfortable fit—what are you, a sausage?" If it was the wrong colour, he had a tie that matched it and made the whole thing work. And if it simply, clearly did not fit at all he'd tell them disgustedly, "You're wearing it wrong."

But I lacked that kind of salesmanship. Even Murray would have found it a tough sell. Beyond that there was still the matter of the hundred dollars and money was always tight enough to squeak in our house.

I had no idea what Arthur made but I remembered him at the kitchen table filling out the application for the parking lot job, and I was shocked that he put down "$400" in the space for "salary expected." Four hundred dollars a month was an outrageous sum, to my mind. If he had that kind of money why were we living in a crappy apartment and driving a little tin-can import car?

I could only assume he'd aimed for the sky and, when the parking lot owners finished laughing and wiped their eyes, had settled for far less when they hired him. But it was becoming evident to me that perhaps four hundred dollars wasn't as much as I'd believed, or else why would he work there then come home and fix stickywindow sashes and broken stove elements?

As simple as "building manager" sounded, as if all you had to do was collect cheques once a month and show empty suites once in a while, that was not the case at all. The phone rang ceaselessly with complaints. My mother dealt with them while Arthur was working at the lot and when he got home he took over. This meant that during the day whatever went wrong beyond burned out lightbulbs was put off until he arrived, and then the fun started. *The door won't close, the door squeaks when it closes, the door won't open. I lost my key, I broke it off in the lock, I used my pocketknife to pry it out and now the blade has broken off in there too, and my hand is bleeding . . . I dropped my keys in the toilet, I dropped my wallet in the toilet, my wig . . .* Arthur was a man of limited handyman skills. It was all he could do to start the lawnmower and when he got his toolkit out from under the sink, anything could happen and very little of it good.

When a tenant moved out and forgot to return the key, the lockset had to be changed. This was an all-day affair with every tool in the box spread out on the carpet and Arthur bleeding from multiple self-inflicted injuries. The finished job was a nightmarish hash of woodwork and doomed attempts to hide the damage with shoe polish or fresh paint. Screws would be sunk so off-centre as to be almost sideways to the wood, the doorframe gouged and scored as if wild beasts had tried to claw their way in, the striker plate on the inside of the jamb actually battered into place with a hammer to get the door to close properly.

This was because Arthur had very little success with the wood chisel and when it failed him, as it was destined to, the hammer was his only resort, the cure-all for any errors in measurement or construction. After hours of failure he would simply bludgeon the recalcitrant parts until they were roughly where they ought to be and then threaten them with an even worse beating if they moved again. Sometimes it worked, mostly because the violence of his workmanship so frightened the tenants they preferred to live with what they had, no matter how crumpled and disfigured, rather than witness another of his attempts at carpentry.

Then there was rent collection day, which was a farce from the start as it always took most of the month to track down and extract the last cheques. There were inside stairwells at the front and back of the buildings and my mother would flush them from one end, like quail, with Arthur waiting at the other to block their escape. When he did corner them they didn't have their chequebook, or the bank had lost their paycheque or the payment on their mother's iron lung was overdue and a million other reasons why they couldn't pay. The phone in our apartment rang constantly with the owners wanting to know where their money was.

So if Arthur was in a permanently disagreeable mood, I suppose you could hardly blame him. No, I needed to make this dog business as painless as I could. Fortunately, once I thought on it, the answer was right in front of me; rather, upstairs. One of the tenants was an immigrant man named Charlie, and he and Arthur could stand in the hall and talk soccer by the hour. As a fairly new arrival in Canada, Charlie was lacking a few household items, among them a TV set. By a stroke of serendipity, we had a spare one in the storage locker. It was technically my TV, a birthday present from my father, a nice little fourteen-inch black and white set with a blonde wood cabinet and skinny wooden legs;

it looked like a one-eyed daddy longlegs designed by Danish modernists.

But there was only one cable jack in the apartment and that was in the living room. Without it, the TV in my room could only bring in a ghostly image of the CBC that wavered in and out of a field of grey and white fuzz and crackling static. Since it was no use to me I was happy to let Charlie have it, and he said when he was making more money he would pay me for it. That was some months back—no doubt he had the money by now. All I had to do was go upstairs and ask him for it. In fact, one hundred dollars for a practically new TV was probably a bargain. I expected he'd pay me on the spot.

That's not quite how it happened. I knocked on his door and told Charlie I needed to get the money for the TV now and gave him my price. Charlie was not especially thrilled by the offer and the conversation was inconclusive. I came back downstairs and continued plotting. Shortly thereafter Charlie was at our door with the set in his arms, thanking us for the loan but saying he couldn't afford it and that we should maybe advertise in the laundry room, or the newspaper. It wasn't long until the story came out and Charlie was sent back upstairs with the set while I was banished to my room to think on what I'd done and the embarrassment I'd caused to both our family and to Charlie. I don't recall what punishment came of it, but it hardly mattered. I'd killed any chance at all of getting my dingo and that was more punishment that I could bear. For days I stopped on my way home and stood outside the pet store and stared at him, my heart breaking anew each time until I could take it no longer and stayed away. One day when I went back, he was finally gone.

Not only was I not getting my dingo, it looked like I had pretty much guaranteed I wouldn't be getting any dog at all. I went through the days in a muzzy, dispirited daze. Spring came and my baseball mitt stayed on the bookshelf in my room while I lay on the bed and escaped into books. I had never had a broken heart before but it seemed to me the sort of thing you didn't ever really recover from. I expected to feel this way the rest of my life. It wasn't so bad—another sixty or seventy years and it would all be over.

I don't think anyone else expected me to recover, either, at least not without help. Some weeks later my mother told me to stay home after school because Arthur was bringing me a present, and I would want to be there the minute it arrived. Despite my despondent state I was intrigued enough to sit out back on the steps and wait for Arthur's little blue Datsun to come bouncing down the alley, and here it came. I ran to the car as he got out, carrying something wrapped in his jacket.

"Here," he said, "this is for you," and he handed the bundle to me. I could smell and feel it even before it poked its head out: a black floppy-eared, curly-haired pup, whining and licking and scrabbling to get to me.

It was the last thing I expected and I had no idea what it was. Its ears hung down past its jawline. My first thought was, we can call him Dumbo.

"She's a cocker spaniel," Arthur said proudly. On the one hand she was cute as could be, with shining black eyes and a wet black nose, and a tiny white blaze on her chest. I loved her immediately, but at the same time my heart sank a little.

I knew that while cocker spaniels were undeniably dogs, but . . . they were the sort of dogs families with infant children had because they were . . . harmless. They were not built for adventure, they could not lope effectively, or spring into action or snarl a warning through slavering jaws or any of the things the dogs I had pictured in my mind could do. The only picture I could summon for a cocker spaniel was of it chasing a butterfly through a meadow while Dick and Jane skipped along behind. I had imagined a fierce but loyal partner, built from the jungle animals in the Tarzan books and the hero dogs on television: shepherds, huskies, Labradors . . . I wanted a wolf and instead I'd been given a lamb.

Part of me was thrilled, part of me was angry, and part of me was ashamed that I was so ungrateful, and all the while the little dog in my arms yipped and barked and licked my neck and face. "She's a girl," I said.

Arthur sensed my less than total joy and said angrily, "Lassie's a girl! What's the matter with you—nothing's good enough for you, is it?" Arthur and I were doomed to never understand or even much like each other. We fought at the drop of a hat, or any other item. It was instinctive and unavoidable and I bear my share of the blame. We were like two dogs who meet on the street and after one sniff of the other, growl and stiffen their legs, ready to fight at the least incitement.

It was also the first time I'd ever encountered the strange idea of giving someone a gift that, while not really what they wanted, suits *you* right down to the ground. I don't believe he did it consciously, but whether he did or simply assumed I'd naturally want the kind of dog he wanted, there we were.

When I couldn't come up with a suitable name for our new dog quickly enough, he did and she was christened Kiltie, a reference to his Scots homeland.

It didn't take long before we all thought of her as Arthur's dog, except when he berated me for not walking "my dog" or taking her to the baseball field with me, but by the time she was old enough to go with me it was clear she was simply not that kind of dog. Her legs were too short to run any distance after a bike and she was likely to get hurt. She was frightened by cars and other dogs and would much rather lay in the kitchen while my mother cooked, or watch TV with Arthur and sneak up onto his lap. They were both very happy and I kept my mouth shut.

*Chapter Three*

# Spooky

Not long after this, when I was in grade six or seven, we moved from Vancouver to White Rock, a small seaside town about as far south on the west coast of Canada as you can go without having to learn the Pledge of Allegiance. We rented a small house that, like almost all of the houses in town, had been built as a summer vacation home and consequently had no insulation. My mother hung blankets between the rooms to keep the heat in and when it was too cold for the cheap baseboard electric heaters to warm the house, we sat around with the oven turned up and its door open.

I made friends with the kids down the alley, Larry and Danny, the Swan brothers. Larry was several years older than Danny and I and had already embarked upon his life's work of theft and vandalism. Mrs. Swan was a single mother who hung onto their little house by her fingernails and tried to stay ignorant of Larry's business as much as possible, to the extent that she would under no circumstances go into the garage or even look through its tiny side window. This enabled her to say, truthfully, "I don't know" and "I didn't see anything" to any questions posed by police or angry neighbours. Meanwhile, Larry was sorting their stolen possessions with Danny and I as lookouts.

The Swans had a dog, too, its name long forgotten, a thin black-and-white, bright-eyed mutt, with great enthusiasm for running behind bikes, chasing cars, fighting, jumping fences and general mischief. I remember him as exceptionally smart, though that may be because in comparison to Danny almost anyone looked good. He was a nice enough kid but thirteen or fourteen years of regular beatings from Larry had surely rattled loose whatever brains he started with. Really, all he had going for him now were thumbs and walking upright.

Kiltie and I were a strange pair to add to this trio, but in childhood you become friends with the only kids on your block whether you like each other or not. We rode bikes, ate popsicles, robbed cherries from the neighbours trees at midnight, read comics, argued and fought—Danny and I—while Larry smoked and laughed, then made up and went back to business as usual. Kiltie sometimes came up the lane with me but the Swans' dog ran frantic circles around her, barking and nipping, until she rolled onto her back and surrendered. She didn't really know how to play much less fight, and the whole business upset her. I was ashamed of her and sent her home.

Spring came and the days lengthened, and we spent

more time further from home, riding our bikes down
to the pier or across the border to buy comics. The
new issues were on the racks in the U.S. weeks ahead of
their appearance in our country, and they had exciting
and strange candy at the checkout stand — chocolate
bars called Abba-Zabba, Big Hunk and Zagnut,
and the unsettling Idaho Spud, a marshmallow-
centred, coconut and chocolate-covered lump that did
look vaguely like a potato but even more like a bowel
movement.

After nearly fifty years the details have melted into a
frames-missing, randomly-spliced montage of pictures
and memories but either Spooky found me or I found
her while out on my bike, alone, somewhere in the far
reaches of White Rock, down at the easternmost end
of town near the Semiahmoo Indian Reserve, which
seems a likely place to find a dog. The Indians did not
subscribe to the spay-and-neuter movement and always had more dogs than they knew what to do with.
On weekends there were always two or three groups
in the IGA parking lot with boxes of puppies for sale.
Whatever the details, I set out alone that day and she
came out of the scrub brush and chased my bike, barking a puppy bark of joy.

So it was that I came back to the house with a light-
brown pup with a dark band across her eyes, like a cartoon burglar's mask. She was a little bear, thick with
puppy fat and tripping over her paws, and clearly insane in the way the best puppies are, full of murder and
delight. She danced and postured at my feet, barked

and snapped at the air, bit mouthfuls of dirt and leaped back in surprise and murdered small sticks, shaking them in her jaws and flinging them into the air. She showed up out of nowhere and laid claim to me, and my recollection is that there was no one around if I had even wanted to return her to wherever she'd come from. This did not make me terribly unhappy and I could tell my mother without a word of a lie that she had followed me home. I can't say for sure, nearly fifty years later, but I don't believe I mentioned that I waited for her when necessary, called her if something threatened to distract or lead her away and carried her across the busier streets.

My mother was a sucker for animals and I knew that once she'd held the pup I was home free. The trick would be getting Arthur to agree but that gave me several hours to work. We didn't need nearly that long. Five minutes after we came through the door Mom was on the floor being licked and leaped on, complaining all the while that this was someone else's dog and we had to call the pound and anyway we already had a dog. But Kiltie loved this little dog too and they chased each other around the house happily while Mom mixed up a bowl of food and warm milk. "Look at those paws," she said, shaking her head. "She's going to be enormous."

It was held as gospel in our family that the size of a puppy's feet were an accurate indicator of how large the dog would be when grown. Dogs seem to be born with their feet already full-grown while the rest of them has to catch up, and most puppy feet look outrageously big compared to their bodies. Kiltie, for one, had paws the size of baked potatoes when her body was roughly the size of a cantaloupe. She ended up about the size of a medium watermelon, and while she never got much longer she did eventually hit prize-winning weight thanks to her impressive begging ability. In my experience the best way to reckon a pup's eventual size is by how much spare skin they have. They arrive in a too-big suit and grow into it like the youngest kid in a large family. Spooky was middlin' baggy and grew up to be low-slung and lean, though she likely would have filled out more in middle-age, as we all do. To my lasting sorrow, that was not to be.

As expected, Arthur put his foot down when confronted with a second dog but he never really had a chance. Spooky went to work on him and by the end of the night she was playing hide-and-seek behind his armchair, jumping out to bark at him when he turned to look the other way and attacking his slipper with comical ferocity. I was to make up telephone-pole Found Puppy flyers and post them after school "without fail," and she could stay until the owners called us. And if they didn't? Then we'd see . . .

I'm sure I did put them up, too. I really wasn't much worried that an owner would appear and demand her back—she had no collar or tags (and if she had I would have thrown them away long before we got home)—and no one did. By the time "we'll see" came around, Spooky was a member of the family.

She grew into a fine young dog, with a majestic, curling, bushy tail that made me think she had husky in her somewhere. Despite my mother's prediction she never became what you could call a big dog—under a hundred pounds and not that tall, though somewhat broad in the shoulder and long-legged for her body. She loved to run and followed me all over town while I searched the spinner racks at various locations, looking for comic books.

Every Wednesday after school I made the rounds, all the way uptown to the Safeway, then back down Johnson Road to the meat of my route, the clump of little stores and druggists at Five Corners, then down the long hill to Marine Drive and along the beach, where pickings were slim but could not be ignored; the one you skipped might be the one that had The Book You Needed. Rain or shine I did the circuit, books wrapped in a plastic bag and zipped inside my coat when it rained, and Spooky always behind me. On nicer days we stopped and shared a chocolate bar or two, in the days before chocolate became poison to dogs and men feared for their blood sugar.

Every evening she went to sleep beside my bed but was always on it by morning when my mother came to wake me. I professed complete innocence of how such a thing might have happened and Spooky rolled sleepily onto her back for stomach scratches.

One of our favourite things to do on weekends was to pack a knapsack full of whatever my mother would donate out of her cupboards, tinned food and cook-

ies and an old cooking pot, and set out overnight for
Crescent Beach. Danny and I would meet up to com-
pare what supplies we'd cadged and head out with our
dogs, first down Buena Vista Avenue to the bottom
of the hill then across Marine Drive and the railroad
tracks onto the beach. From there we headed for the
jut of coastline to the west, roughly halfway to Crescent Beach, around the other side of the peninsula.
There was nothing there that we didn't have right
where we were, but the sun was shining and it was
something to do.

Within the first few miles there were no longer
houses on the other side of the tracks, only thick woods
and bramble. The dogs could run and chase seagulls
on the sand and in the water, and we could throw drift-
wood into the shallows for them. When we got tired
we stopped and made a fire in the shelter of the great
rocks that elevated the railroad tracks what now seems
in memory to be hundreds of feet above the ground
beside the beach, though it was really only six or so
when I went back to look at it last summer.

The sun came down and slid behind the ocean and
we made our dinner, canned stew or beans and spam
with Kool-Aid from the thermos. The dogs curled up
by the fire and we unrolled our sleeping bags. The sun-
set lasted for a while in mid-summer and by the time it
was fully dark we were all asleep, my bag unzipped at
the side so Kiltie and Spooky could snuggle in.

The stars filled the sky and waves lapped at the sand
and in the morning we woke to the smell of salt and

rotting seaweed, a strange, rich, and pungent odour. Anywhere else it would turn your stomach but on the beach you fill your lungs with it, as if you were standing outside the doughnut shop, except for the sand fleas jumping at your feet.

We rolled our bags up and hoisted our knapsacks and decided to take the tracks for a while. It was less interesting but we could make better time walking on the railroad ties than pushing through the damp sand. There's a tiny film clip in my mind of what happened then that still shames me every time I replay it.

Were we on the trestle bridge? It's the only thing that makes sense. How else could we have let a train sneak up on us? The engineers highballed it through that lonely stretch, and if we had taken the bridge rather than climb over the rocks back down to the sand, we would have been trapped on it when the train saw us and its whistle screamed. That's how I remember it, the bridge just that much too high to leap off it to safety, and anyway, the dogs would never jump. Instead they ran behind us, unable to go very fast without falling through.

We could smell the train, the smoking oil and grinding hot metal, as the wheels shrieked and the whistle sounded loud as the judgement horn. Danny and I made it to the far end and jumped to the sides and I shouted for Spooky to come while Kiltie ran behind her, eyes wide in terror, tongue hanging out of the side of her mouth. She was not built for speed and she was running for her life. I grabbed Spooky and yanked her to the side as she crossed the last tie and then at the last possible moment Kiltie jumped off the track as the train howled and clattered past and I felt the first sharp pains of an embarrassment so deep I can barely write it down.

I had not been concerned with Kiltie at all. I didn't want her to be hurt, or killed as she most certainly would have been, but in the heat of it my attention had been focused on getting Spooky to safety and it was Spooky whom I was hugging and crying tears of relief over. It was her that I had yelled for while poor Kiltie ran her race with death, and was much more likely to lose. She was a sweet, loving dog and the only thing she had ever done wrong was to simply not be the dog I wanted. She could do no more about that than I could, though she tried. She followed us on bikes and on foot until her own little pads were worn raw and still she wanted to come along. I have never forgiven myself and I doubt I ever will.

Later that summer my mother arranged for us to visit a friend of hers from back in the housing project, who'd also met a new man and escaped. They were in Calgary and it was going to be a long drive. Too long a trip for two dogs and three people in one small car. There's a car ad that says "In life, there are drivers and there are passengers," and Spooky was somewhere in between. While Kiltie would curl up and snooze in the Datsun, Spooky moved from one window to another, barking and growling at dogs in other cars and certain motorists she had her doubts about. She loved it and I was thoroughly entertained but the grownups were not about to suffer nearly seven hundred miles and fifteen hours of her exuberance.

I didn't exactly lose the argument. It was one time when there was none, really. They teamed up on me and buried me under an avalanche of inarguable logic. "It's too far for her to go in a car—she needs to get out and run and we can't stop that often, and there isn't room for both of them, and Kiltie would be so lonely but Spooky can stay with the Swans until we get back and she'll have lots of fun with the boys and we'll be back before you know it."

And so one July morning we set out in our little car and went exactly one half-block up the alley where I handed Spooky and her bag of food over to Danny and hugged her neck and told her I'd be back soon and to be good.

I never saw her again. We came back two weeks later and I wanted to be let off up the road so I could bring her home. I got out of the car and Mrs. Swan told me that Spooky had been hit by a car the day after we left. Danny said she simply ran out into the street and there was nothing he could do, but that was the end of our friendship. Every time I saw him I was filled with more hate and grief than a thirteen-year-old should be able to hold. If I had to fix a date to it, I would say that my childhood ended there. God is no respecter of persons, nor of dogs, and he has much to answer for.

Kiltie lived several more years after I left home but I saw her and Muggins the cat only when I came back to eat or beg. She was never really my dog anyway and I feel far worse about that than she ever did. Long before I was gone she spent her days on my stepfather's recliner waiting for him to get home, got off it briefly to welcome him, and then got back up into his lap to be fed bits of whatever until it was time for bed. She was cossetted—a word from the sixteenth century that meant a lamb kept as a pet, overly indulged and fondled—and became very fat. She had to be picked up and set down, and he called her "my lady" when he was cross with her, as in, "Och, my lady, look what you've done," while he brushed her stray hairs off his pants in mock annoyance.

Then he would go to the closet, with her waddling behind him like a seal across the rocks, and spend fifteen minutes getting into coat, scarf, gloves, shoes, and cap before taking her out to do her business, as he called it, while she danced at his feet. Or rocked really, side-to-side from one foot to the other. Then he snapped on her leash, as if she were going to run off without it, and away they went, dawdling into the night, down to the end of the block and back. In winter he took a flashlight with him, just in case. The Apollo moon missions took less gear along on their excursions and made better time.

It seems as if I were only gone from the house a short while but it must have been two years or more when my mother came one day to take me to the dentist. Years earlier I had broken a front tooth playing sports and over the years it had gotten progressively worse, and now needed to be rebuilt. It was an ugly business, requiring a metal post be screwed into my jaw for the new tooth to be affixed to, and done with much yanking and twisting with what looked more to me like tools from a mechanic's bench than the delicate instruments one expects a dentist to use. On the trip home, through a haze of pain killers and nitrous oxide, I asked how the animals were.

"Oh, we had them put down," she said. She was rather blasé about it, seeming to me no more emotional than she would be about going through the Tupperware containers in the fridge and discarding some peas that had been in there a little too long.

I was furious.

"Jesus Christ! Did you just wake up one morning and decide to kill them? Did you get a better price if you did the two of them?" In my defense, it was a bit much to hear the news like that, with a mouth full of bloody cotton batting.

"Oh no, dear. They were old and sick," my mother said.

I remember resting my face against the cold window of the car and how it felt against my swollen, half-frozen mouth. It was quite a few years later that I came to believe her. In my mind the animals should have stayed the way they were when I left and ought to still be just that way whenever I came by again, as if they had been kept vacuum-packed and only taken out for special occasions. But the truth is that at the end of a life the years rush by as if they'd been tossed down a steep hill, picking up speed the nearer they get to the end, and not just for dogs and cats. It happens to parents with the same brutal speed, between one Christmas visit and the next.

# Chapter Four

# Chopper

I had no pets of my own over the next five or six years. I was trying to be a musician and could barely feed myself. I might be gone for days when I went out the door.

I lived first with my friend Art in an apartment in White Rock, in a building across the street from the ocean. The place had been built for summer rental and the large windows in the front rooms slid completely open. You could throw an empty beer bottle through them out over the small rise of the railroad tracks and hit the beach. Seagulls would perch on the open sill and accept pieces of toast.

Art's dog Chopper was in semi-retirement at Art's parent's home in Cloverdale. He was a great black-and-brown beast of uncertain heritage with a broad, square head and a short, wide snout, and ears that were, simply, ears, one to a side. He had no pretensions — he looked like a dog, he smelled like one, and he did dog things. He liked to be outside digging and investigating but he also loved to be in the centre of the party where people had one hand on their drink and the other absently scratching the dog at their side. He liked beer, which he acquired a taste for at an early age, and he loved parties, because at parties everyone gave him beer. He was a good dog but a bad drunk, given to picking fights. Even when sober he chased cars and barked at noises. It's no wonder we all loved him. He behaved just like we did.

He was living with Art in an old house when I first met him but they had gone separate ways when Art found this apartment. He often visited though, when Art's brother or friends brought him over. When he did I took him hunting late at night, when the party was over. I took a beer or two that had been hidden away and we prowled the seaside alleys, looking for cats. When Chopper saw one he launched himself with surprising velocity for a dog that really wasn't designed for any kind of speed. For short bursts, though, he could race with the best of them.

The cats always had the same surprised look on their faces. Here it was, long after midnight, and time for a leisurely stroll along a fence and a look-see inside certain un-lidded garbage cans, and into this genteel setting comes a roaring beast with red glowing eyes and slavering jaws, howling and snapping. Away they went down the alley, through garbage cans and old balsa-wood crates and boxes until the cat made it over a fence or through a hole and Chopper came back wheezing and trailing drool. It sounds evil, but the cats were in no danger of being caught and the high intensity cardiovascular workout can only have done them good. They should have thanked us, really.

Chopper needed the exercise, too. While he was living at the house in Cloverdale he had discovered an all-you-can-eat buffet next door at the junior high school that abutted the Bergmann home. When he heard the bell Chopper made tracks for the school and looked for a likely victim. There were plenty to choose from; the students were very casual about their sand-wiches and cookies between bites, dangling them from their fingers, arms at their sides, and Chopper was like a whale traversing the open sea, jaws agape and sifting plankton, except that he approached from the rear, sa-liva falling from his muzzle, padding silently across the pea-gravel of the yard. Then he sprang. One great leap and he snatched the food and was gone, swallowing as he ran. The student screamed, understandably, and his friends all laughed. If they were in a group, the ones who could see Chopper coming became collaborators, traitors to their species, and tried not to give the game away.

It was just too much fun to see that enormous mouth and flash of teeth, and the surgeon-like precision of the chomp, and the accompanying shriek of terror. When I say surgeon-like, I mean exactly that—Chopper never once took a finger. He could separate the sand-wich from the hand with speed and precision. Then he was gone again, around the corner to the other side of the building and whatever delicacies awaited there.

Around and around he went, until the bell called the students back inside and Chopper trotted home.

They weren't all little apple-cheeked moppets—some of them threw rocks that Chopper tried to catch like a Frisbee and his front teeth became broken and ragged. It didn't deter him though—he elevated his game and began stealing the whole lunch bag, bringing them home like prizes to the door, where Mrs. Bergmann picked the meat out of the sandwiches for him.

It was this that led to Chopper's banishment from Cloverdale. An administrator from the school knocked on the Bergmanns' door one day and told them they would have to do something about the dog before someone was hurt. Fortunately we had found a new place to live, a century-old farmhouse some miles east of White Rock proper, with a field on either side and woods in the back. We could make all the noise we liked there and generally do as we pleased, and so could Chopper.

It was an enormous old wreck of a place and a ridiculous bargain for us. The lady who had owned it was keeping company with the widowed father of our friend Murphy. Ever since she inherited the place it had been a constant source of stress, what with the insurance costs for an empty property, the vandalism and broken windows, the property taxes and no income from it. I don't know why it wasn't just rented out—maybe it was simply too old and ramshackle and too far from everything else. In the movies, it would be the home of a clan of cannibal hillbillies, skinning unwary motorists for window shades and making jerky out of the meat. But I suppose that represented a very small portion of the tenancy market in the real world, and so Murphy's father suggested she give the place to "the boys" in exchange for keeping the place safe and paying the taxes. We moved in before she'd finished saying yes.

It was a very reasonable price and that was good because we couldn't afford any more. There was no shortage of gigs for our various bands to play but they all tended to pay in free drinks and other valuable but non-negotiable forms of tender. Mostly we were dead broke, and on occasion close to starving. Chopper would go with me to search the ditches for pop cans and bottles up and down the long stretch of North Bluff Avenue that ran in front of the house. It was good hunting usually, and within a few miles we found enough to walk back to the store at Pacific Highway and cash them in for a couple of boxes of macaroni and cheese dinner, Chopper sitting outside the store, tongue hanging, while I attended to business at the counter. Then back home to cook it up with Chopper licking the pot to a high gleam afterwards.

I honestly don't know what he got fed, other than random table scraps. He did head off into the woods by himself and come back hours later, tired and filthy. We assumed he found things and ate them. There was a mental home on one side of us, several hundred yards away and across a small creek and ravine, and Chopper wandered over there sometimes and often brought a patient home with him.

One afternoon when Art was home alone Chopper cornered an unfortunate critter under the front porch, a dark crawlspace that no one would ever willingly crawl into short of nuclear war. There was much snarling and shrieking and when he came out with the limp thing in his jaws, it was hard to tell what sort of animal it had been. While Chopper was gnawing on the corpse some horrible parasite crawled out of the guts, "like a huge white grub," Art said later. Chopper ate that, too. Art was clearly disturbed by the whole business and so was I. Living in the country gives you a much different perspective on nature than watching it on the Discovery Channel.

Chopper had no problems with killing and neither did I as it turned out. At one point we were living on a massive sack of potatoes and flats of rejected eggs that someone had brought home from a poultry farm. They were either fertilized or so misshapen and malformed they would scare the retail customers, so they were culled and marked for destruction. Instead, they wound up in our refrigerator. Most of them were edible, if you were hungry enough, and we were. Chopper ate the other ones, fertilized chicken embryos and all.

It didn't take long to get truly sick of eggs but that gastronomic ennui did not extend to chickens themselves. One wandered into our yard one day and I was out of my chair and looking for a blunt instrument without hesitation. Axes are the professional's preferred instrument for chicken murder but we had none. I settled for a length of two-by-four.

Chopper was all too willing to help and he pounced and snapped happily while I chased the poor, terrified thing around the yard waving the leg from a broken chair. I dealt it many glancing blows but it took more than an hour to finally run it down and deliver the *coup de grace*, several of them actually. It clucked its last, finally, and lay there battered and still.

Now the question was what to do with the meat? Somewhere I remembered reading that the pioneers used wax to strip the feathers off. We had candles and it sounded simple enough. I melted some down and poured the hot wax over the chicken in the sink. The theory was that the wax cooled around the feathers and then you pulled the whole business off with no bother at all. Well, people supposedly wove ropes out of grass and sewed animal skins into clothing with thorns for needles, and I doubt that worked worth a damn either. I was left with a dead chicken covered in wax and a fine coat of waterproof feathers; I was trying to make dinner and instead I'd built a duck.

I began to pull the feathers out one by one, made all the more difficult by the slippery wax coating. It took a very long time and while I got most of the feathers off eventually, the bird was still covered in wax. I soaked it in hot water but that just spread the wax thinly and more evenly. I scrubbed its hide with a shoe brush and finally admitted defeat. Time to put it in the pot.

None of our knives would cut through the sinew at

the joints but I hacked at it with increasing frenzy until it finally came apart in serial-killer shreds and chunks. It needed another good cleaning when I was done, and so did I. Back in the sink, then into a pot with some water and potatoes and a little salt and pepper. Get the heat nice and high and boil the hell out of it. A sudden inspiration and a search for pennies and then down the road for an onion at the store. When I got back it was beginning to smell like food.

All the while Chopper was keeping close to the kitchen, lying in the doorway to the back entry. This was clearly not any regular sort of cooking but it was still worth keeping an eye on.

It was hard to ignore the smell of my stew as it bubbled away. The liquid was a little thin, granted, but there were definite hints of onion and chicken in there and the starch from the potatoes gave it a bit of body. More of a soup than a stew really, and not much of a soup at that, to be honest. But as my grandmother said, "hunger makes good sauce." When I'd waited as long as I could I dished up a bowl of it and retired to the table, blowing on it and spooning up that first piece of chicken, mindful of the shattered bone fragments.

I put the first piece of steaming chicken into my mouth and sucked air around it desperately. Then I bit down, and the chicken bit back. There was a definite resistance one did not normally associate with stewed chicken. I bit harder and my jaws sprang back with a force that was positively Newtonian. This was not right, not right at all.

I took the thing out of my mouth and poked it with the fork. The tines made a dent but didn't actually penetrate, like someone attempting to give Superman a hypodermic injection. I got a knife from the drawer, a piece of cutlery I hadn't expected to need. I could saw a piece off, but not easily, and I still couldn't chew it once I had it separated. I might has well have boiled up a tire with some onion and potatoes.

Also, as it cooled, a fine film of wax formed on the top of the bowl. You could suck on the chicken but it didn't really have much of a flavour, chicken or otherwise. What I really had was an onion and potato broth lightly seasoned with chicken and wax, with some ornamental chunks of meat.

It was very discouraging. I put the bowl on the floor and gave Chopper the signal. He cleaned it up in seconds. What he couldn't chew, he swallowed whole.

(It was the most depressing cooking experience of my life, matched only by the Christmas I tried to cook a turkey drumstick over the steam spout of an electric kettle in the tiny rented room I was living in.

"Are you cooking in there?" the manager shouted through the door.

"No, not really," I yelled back.)

Chopper loved car rides and when our housemate Slim bought an old white pickup, Chopper would sit in the truckbed for hours in case someone decided to go for a drive, though he actually considered it more of a taxi service than a round-trip excursion; he was known to leap out of the car and light out for the territories if the mood struck him. Art recalls him jumping out once around Abbotsford as they slowed for a corner and coming home to the house in Cloverdale three days later, a distance of forty miles or so, limping down the driveway with a "You should see the other guy" grin on his face. When he took off you were worried about him, but equally concerned for the unsuspecting world he'd been loosed on. He truly seemed indestructible so it was hard to believe when he was killed chasing a car some years later. He'd lost a step or two, I imagine, as all the great ones do eventually, but he died doing what he loved, and that's the important thing. I always wondered about the car, though. I would bet he fought it to a draw.

*Chapter Five*

# Rip

Rip was a dog, there was no doubt about it, but beyond that your guess is as good as mine. There was
probably shepherd in there, somewhere, but the simplest way to describe him is that he was half pig and
half bear, and somehow still all dog.

At first look, he seemed to have been made from
parts left over when making all the other dogs of the
world, and when you looked again you just became
more convinced of it. His shoulders were enormous
and his chest was fit for pulling wagons, but he tapered
severely down to the shanks like a cartoon bodybuilder,
and this over-inflated torso was set on legs that managed to be both stumpy and delicate. He started off
silver-white and black with light brown highlights in
early youth but over the years he became a sort of indeterminate, faded, tan colour speckled with white and
grey, like a man's late-middle-age beard. It's odd that I
can't describe the colour better—I had enough opportunity to study it. Rip lived for more than sixteen years
and for another decade after his death we were still
finding his hair. Calling it "hair" is insufficient—they

were more like quills from a porcupine and seemed to be barbed in some fashion, like a spirochete, so that when they penetrated a couch cushion or a sweater they slid into the material like they were oiled and stuck there with the tenacity of burrs when you tried to pull them out.

Eventually certain blankets and throws were so covered with Rip hair there was nothing for it but to just give them up to him and say, "Oh, that's just a Rip blanket now." Trying to reclaim the thing was ridiculous—it would have required something on the order of electric sheep-shears or a tiny lawn mower. But since he slept on the bed and lay on the couch with us too, any blanket we shared was doomed to become Rip's, not that he needed or wanted it. Why would he, when he was up on the bed or the couch with us? This was in my drinking days, and I spent more time on the floor than he did; if anyone slept with the Rip blankets, it was me.

Most people choose furniture to match the carpets or the draperies or to fit some scheme—when we bought the first new couch of our lives, we bought it to match the dog. It was an extravagance; we could have simply upholstered the old one in his stray hair. Rip had a thick coat at all times but from the amount of hair he lost you would think he'd been peeled like an orange. A friend joked that if he got lost we could just knit a spare one from the hair on the floorboards and behind the doors. You could sweep several times a day, not that we did.

This may in fact have been a genetic survival trait.

There was no five-second or one-bounce rule in our house. If it hit the deck, it was Rip's. There was no argument at all. After only glancing contact with the floor it looked like a small rodent, whatever it was to begin with, and he was welcome to it.

Like Moses in the rushes, Rip was a foundling. A friend discovered him when she was walking her own dog, an enormous shepherd named Timber. She worked at a hospital laundry and her day started at six in the morning so she took Tim out before she left, and while passing a Safeway on a cold Vancouver morning in March 1983 he pulled her across the parking lot to a cardboard box. Inside it, wrapped in a T-shirt, was a gerbil-sized Rip, all feet and wrinkles in a dog suit several sizes too big for him. His eyes were still closed and he was very unhappy. She bundled him into her own coat and came straight home where she swaddled him in old sweaters and towels in a new box, and fed him condensed milk and sugar from an eyedropper. She came by later in the day and showed him to my girlfriend.

By the time I got home from work, I had a dog.

I didn't regret it for a minute over the next sixteen years. My wife-to-be Mary and I lived in a tiny two-bedroom apartment that was maybe five hundred square feet in total, if you counted the stairwell. We'd been there for five years and might have stayed another five if it hadn't been for Rip. It was clear very quickly that we needed more room. He went from a blind, whimpering lump of fur to actual little dog in short order, and from wobbling to racing in the wink of an eye. He ran from one room to the other, which was not much of a trip, and skidded around corners into chairs, garbage cans, doors, record albums stacked against walls, and us, then bounced off, roaring away in a new direction. But all roads led back in that apartment and here he came again, yipping and tumbling and down to the bottom of the stairs and back up again to stop and stare at us, panting, with a mad look in his eye. Then a strange, spastic, simultaneous head-fake and butt-wriggle and he launched himself again at full speed. Halfway across the room he would stop suddenly and pass out, dropping to the floor as if shot, and remain that way, oblivious, for several minutes — he only had two speeds: escape velocity and catatonia.

He slept on the bed between us, smelling the way all puppies smell, as if they'd been rolled in cornflakes. Sometime during the night I'd hear the thump as he jumped/fell off the bed, then the thump of little feet as he headed out to his paper and peed, then the whine that meant he wanted back up, and I would reach down and lift him up into the sleeping bag where he would burrow in between us again. There was only room for a twin-sized mattress in that bedroom, and it was clear that very soon it would not be big enough for Rip, much less the three of us.

By the time Rip was six months old we found a house for rent with a fenced yard and for the next fifteen years every time I moved I went through the same anxiety as

I searched the ads looking for a place that would accept a dog. When I did, I was at their mercy—some landlords charged an additional month's rent as pet deposit, some charged more. What could you do? The only alternative was to give the dog up, and that was unthinkable. I'd sleep in a box, in the alley, first.

Before I go further I should explain how he got his name. There's an episode of the original *Twilight Zone* where an old mountain man is out hunting with his dog Rip and they tree a coon. The coon pulls the dog into the river underneath the tree and the old man goes in after them, as a coon will hold the dog under and drown him. Hours later they waken on the riverbank and head home where his wife refuses to talk to him or even acknowledge his presence. It shortly becomes apparent the wife is getting ready for a funeral and . . . exactly.

Considering what to do now that he's dead, the man and dog head down the road and soon find themselves by a gated entry to a massive field. The gatekeeper checks his clipboard and explains that this here is the "Eee-leesian Fields" and we been waiting on you, neighbour, so come right in. Your dog will have to stay outside though . . .

The old man shakes his head and allows that any place that's too fancy for Rip is likely too fancy for him, too, and they set back out on the road where they shortly meet another fellow, who says he's been looking for these two all over creation so he could lead them to the Heavenly Pastures. When the old man explains they've just come from there, the guide tells him he's had a narrow escape. "That was the Devil himself back there, trying one last time to trick an honest, god-fearin' man. But there was never any real danger because a man, well, he'll walk right into Hell with both eyes open. But even the Devil can't fool an old coon-huntin' dog."

Rip seemed like a fine name, and I figured I could use all the help I could get avoiding damnation.

*Chapter Six*

# A Two-Dog Family

Somehow in the years between when Rip arrived and Mary left, I got out of the music business and into journalism. My wife was not particularly pleased with this but Rip was all in. I was making a steady pay-cheque as a reporter for the local paper and that meant I could afford to rent a place with a big fenced yard. She went back to music and I got custody of Rip in the separation.

I moved several times over the next few years but rentals that would let you keep your dog were increasingly hard to find and so, when my mother died in the early nineties and I received a small amount of money, I decided to buy a home. I say "small amount" because even though I had a good job and cash money in hand, Vancouver was then going through one of its recurring "bubbles" and when I told real estate agents I had thirty thousand dollars and wanted to buy a house they laughed, and when they stopped laughing they said, "No, you want to buy an apartment."

Maybe it was genetic memory, a holdover from our

Irish tenant background, all the farms my family had owned briefly and lost to the bank and all the lousy places I'd lived in since leaving home, but I didn't want an apartment. I wanted something where you walked out your door and there was dirt and rocks and grass, not carpet and an elevator. And that meant I could only buy in what was called, with subtle irony, Mount Pleasant.

In earlier times it was surely a pleasant little community, with tree-lined streets and ladies in hoopskirts sipping lemonade while men rode their velocipedes down the wooden sidewalk, tipping their bowler hats as they passed. Now it was crack and whores and Asian-immigrant gangs and low-cost rental housing, the lovely old houses walled off into multiple welfare and disability-cheque apartments.

I found a 1920s Craftsman Cottage that fit my budget for the bargain price of $225,000. I didn't even like to think about that number, nearly a quarter of a million dollars for a little house in a bad neighbourhood, but also I felt very successful—it was easily five times the amount of money anyone in my family had ever owed.

Years later, when my Uncle John was helping me work on the attic he pointed out how the rafters of the building were spaced farther and farther apart as you looked down to the rear of the place. "They were running out of wood," he said, pointing to the spaces between the rafters. "They start off at sixteen inches and by the time you hit the back wall they're nearly two feet apart." Regardless, the roof had held for over eighty years and the cedar was now petrified and bending drywall screws as we attempted to put them in. It was wrong, he said, but it was also permanent, which describes much of life.

There was another reason the house was priced so low, by Vancouver standards; the lady who lived there had bought it a year earlier and been terrorized since the day she moved in. More than once she'd woken up to hear people in the hallway outside her bedroom, laughing and talking as they checked out her belongings and rooted through cupboards. It would have been worth her life to confront them and the cops were famous for non-attendance at break-ins, at least in this neighbourhood. As far as they were concerned, the sooner all the residents murdered each other the better. In fact, after we took possession we called in once looking for the vice squad because we were having problems with the whores next door turning tricks in our car and leaving condoms and used needles on the seats. We were advised to call back in the morning—"the vice squad doesn't work nights."

Even so, we were undeterred. One of the roommates moving in with me was Jason Findlay, a friend from the journalism world and a good man to have handy if things turned ugly. Jason was a strapping six-footer who liked strong drink and martial arts. He'd already learned bar fighting techniques growing up back home in Rugby, Warwickshire, a town famous for hard men—even the hairdressers will kick your ass. As might be guessed, Rugby is where they invented the infamous game with minimal rules and maximum injuries, and where they think playing it is genuinely good fun. Ten years of playing sleazy bars and cultivating bad companions had also toughened me considerably, and I had Rip as well. So let them come — but leave a forwarding address so we can notify the next of kin.

Still, the first thing I did when I got the place was build a fence, a six-foot enclosure on all four sides. It may have seemed a bit extreme but one of the first mornings I woke up there I went into the living room with my coffee, looked out the front window and watched a man shooting up under a tree in the front yard. I borrowed the money for the fence and made sure that both gates locked from the inside, and if anyone cared to climb over it, Rip was on duty in the yard.

He was a fine watchdog and he enjoyed his work, so much so that he wouldn't bark when someone gave the gate handle an exploratory wiggle. He just crouched there, with a deep, low growl in his throat, almost like the purr of an enormous cat, his tail wagging slowly back and forth in anticipation. He was an optimist and always had his hopes up, and they were sometimes rewarded.

Once I heard a shriek from the backyard and went out onto the porch to see a man hanging from the inside lip of the side fence with Rip patiently waiting below. I imagine he vaulted over and saw the dog just in time to swing his feet back up, but now he was stuck there hanging sort of sidewise by his hands like a man doing a pullup, with one foot hooked over the top and the other drawn up to his chest, just out of reach of Rip so long as his arm muscles held out. It didn't look very comfortable.

"Help," he said.

I thought about it for a second. "You got in on your own, you can get out the same way," I said, and went back inside. A few minutes later I heard noises and barking and went back out. He was gone and Rip was running back and forth along the fence, trying to find a way to go after him. Rip had either lost his patience and jumped for him, thereby encouraging him over the hurdle, or fear and adrenaline had enabled him to simply levitate to the other side, like a yogi. Either way, he was gone and I hoped he would spread the word.

The house next door was one of the worst in the neighbourhood, a three-storey stucco and wood home that had been sectioned off into apartments by the landlord, who rented to anyone who could come up with the deposit and keep a straight face when they filled out the "occupation" section on the application. I had already rented out my own basement to a single mother on welfare, a 250-pound woman with an equally oversized ten-year-old. The day she moved in she told me, "I have to be honest with you. I'm in a twelve-step program."

"Good for you," I said. After all, who was I to cast aspersions? I learned soon enough that it would have been more accurate for her to say that she was often in a recovery program and just as often not in it. Almost immediately after moving in she met a man at one of her meetings and he moved in with her and the boy. He seemed a decent enough sort, really, but he must have been very wicked in a previous life to have merited the punishment he was getting in this one. They fell off the wagon constantly, actually more of a broad jump from what I heard through the floorboards. Much screaming and weeping and slamming of doors followed, some of it spilling out into the backyard. Once I heard her howling threats at him and went outside to ask her to stop. From the porch I could see her squatting on the grass peeing, never missing a beat as she hurled abuse and bitter complaints. She pulled up her panties and stretchy pants, wobbling uncertainly and looking as if she were about to sit down in her own mess, than waddled back into the house still shouting. If I were him, I'd be taking all the drugs I could get my hands on, too.

The house next door had teenage Vietnamese gangsters in the basement suite, a collection of hookers on the main floor, and a crack dealer and his prostitute wife on the top. Most of them were outside or at their windows, demanding my tenant shut up. We had managed to annoy the worst neighbours in the world. It was quite an accomplishment, and there was always the possibility that they might get mad enough to kill her and dispose of the body. One could only hope.

But it was not to be. Soon enough both my downstairs neighbours were next door on a regular basis to score drugs and one day I found her sobbing in the backyard. "He's dead, he's dead," she kept saying. They'd been partying with the whores and at some point her boyfriend had decided to spice things up and shoot some cocaine. He had a massive heart attack, which he might have recovered from if the rest of the people in the room had called an ambulance. Instead they spent several hours debating what to do, whether to move him back to my house to avoid police at their own door, whether he'd pull out of it on his own and other important questions. Meanwhile the drinking and crack smoking continued, and he died in the armchair he'd collapsed in and stayed there until morning when someone finally called the medics. "I blame myself," she said, and seemed a little miffed that she got no argument. She began bawling again and I helped her into her apartment.

She appeared at my door a few hours later canvassing for donations to erect a headstone monument for her dead lover. I gave her twenty dollars and she kept us awake the rest of the night with a wake that comprised most of the people who'd helped kill the man the night before.

But I was a home-and-dog-owning taxpayer, the master of my castle, even if I was unable to get rid of my tenant. It was hard for me to imagine a situation in which I was the standard for sobriety and sanity, but here I was. Mobsters and hookers to one side, crazed dope fiend bitch in the basement and me planting trailing lobelia and pansies in the windowboxes. With enough beer it was mostly bearable and the young gangsters next door were smart enough not to steal from the local houses. They really only used the basement suite next door as a clubhouse and a place to store and portion out their goods. And that was how Mugsy came into my life.

Our life, I should say. I met a woman named Lynda who loved animals as much as I did, and she moved in with me. She loved Rip and my old cat Bumstead almost as much as I did.

Bumstead had been with me through the punk rock years and learned to eat Kraft dinner and ramen noodle soups that sold three for a dollar. He was a tough old black-and-white tuxedo cat, and we had a strange relationship. He ignored me, mostly, and I let him alone. We were like neighbours who nod over the fence at each other for twenty years and while we acknowledged each other when we passed in the hall or the kitchen, we didn't make a big fuss out of the occasion. When I was feeling particularly sentimental I'd buy him a can of sliced mushrooms from the corner store and pet him while he ate them. That was our little family, just the four of us.

One day I came home from work to see a Rottweiler pup the gangster boys next door had acquired. From the porch I could see this beautiful brown and black dog chained to a tree in the side yard, with nowhere to go to escape the sun and nothing to drink for who knew how long. I took a pan of water over to him and he jumped all over me. It was very, very hard to leave him there and I nearly unchained him and took him with me. That seemed like a bad plan though so I decided to call the SPCA if they didn't smarten up.

It was a good thing I had left him there. One of the guys was standing in the yard behind me. "You like dog?" he asked. "Purebred, five grand. You want him?"

"Not for five thousand dollars, I don't. You got papers for him?"

He looked puzzled. "Papers? Guy is abusing him. Kick shit out of him, we take dog. No papers."

"Well, purebred or not if you don't have papers he's just a dog. You're not going to get five grand for him."

He thought about that for second but it was too much for him. "Fuck you," he said.

I left the negotiation there and went home. Lynda or I made sure he had water and food from then on and over the next few days the problem took care of itself.

The boys in the basement were buying crack on credit from the dope dealer upstairs, a small, muscular black man named Stan. Eventually Stan came downstairs looking for a little something on account and, outnumbering him about five to one, they advised him to fuck off. Lynda and I were having a beer on the back porch and had a fine view of the proceedings.

We heard angry voices from the basement suite and then Stan came back out and up the three or four steps into the yard. We were somewhat friendly with

Stan—it seemed a much better idea than not being friends with him—and asked him what was up.

Stan picked up a short length of scrap wood from the garbage in the backyard and said, "Just evicting some Chinamen." Back he went down the steps and through the door. Immediately there were screams in Vietnamese and my mind flashed back to Walter Cronkite and black-and-white war footage on the *CBS Evening News*, then I heard heavy thuds like someone beating a carpet and the sounds of furniture overturning and glass breaking. One of them scrambled through the basement window and ran for the front yard but Stan laid him out with three or four smart whacks of his justice log, then walked back casually.

"Want a beer?" we said and threw him one over the fence.

Stan twisted the cap off and looked around. Two or three of the Vietnamese limped to their car and left while he watched. "They owe me five hundred bucks," he said, "and all they had was this dog. You want a purebred Rotti?"

I wasn't going to get into that again and just said, "I would but I can't afford it." Within a week Stan dropped the price to fifty dollars. As part of my good-neighbour program I'd lent him small amounts of money on occasion. I went in the house and asked Lynda if she had a five, then I went next door and held it out to Stan and said, "I gave you twenty bucks twice last month and another five for cigarettes a couple of days ago. So this makes fifty and we're square. All right?"

He thought about it for a second then sighed and took the bill.

"Goddamn it, that dog's worth five thousand dollars," he said, folding up the five and putting it in his pants.

He was worth far more than that. We had no intentions of keeping him and when I brought him back to our yard my first words to Lynda were, "We'll find him a good home. The last thing we need is a vicious Rottweiler."

That phrase became a running joke over the years. Stan said his name was Fritz but when we called him that it just sounded wrong. He was no more Fritz than I was Mabel. Lynda came up with Mugsy and once she said it out loud we knew it was right. That night he jumped onto the bed beside Lynda as if to say, *I'm not going anywhere.*

And he wasn't; it took about an hour for him to banish any ideas we had about "vicious Rottweilers." He was, to be honest, about as threatening as a teddy bear and had no more violence in him than a caterpillar. I was deeply confused by this; all I knew about the breed was what I'd seen in movies where they guarded junkyards and prison camps, a bigger, stronger, nastier version of the Doberman. Not Mugsy. In terms of evil Germans, he was right up there with Sergeant Schultz. We bought a book at the pet store that said:

> The Rottweiler's ancestors were drover's dogs accompanying the cattle herds the Romans brought with them when invading Europe. Their herding and

guarding instincts were recognized by the Germans, and dogs were selectively bred for these traits, resulting in two "races", a larger one for cart pulling and a smaller one to herd cattle and guard. Rottweilers love their people and may behave in a clownish manner toward family and friends, but they are also highly protective of their territory.

Mugsy would have been a cart puller, which was fine because Rip did enough guarding for both of them, though they made an impressive and discouraging pair for anyone thinking about breaking in. He was maybe six months old and already more than two feet tall at the shoulder, with a powerful neck and massive head. He was huge, sweet, and mostly clueless, about 120 pounds and not a lot of it between his ears. He was so big, in fact, that he didn't even need to do any active "guarding"; it was enough to just stand there.

When he was about a year old I came downstairs and saw Mugsy standing in front of the large window that looked out onto the front porch. On the other side of it was a disreputable-looking guy with his jacket wrapped around his fist and forearm. It wasn't hard to deduce he'd been just about to break the window, thinking no one was home, when Mugsy rose up from the floor like some great monster from the depths of the ocean. The break-in artist was a skinny little fellow and Mugsy likely had ten or twenty pounds on him, and while not quite as tall, had much larger teeth. Neither of them was doing anything at the moment. They were so quiet that Rip hadn't heard anything and was still upstairs watching TV with Lynda. Mugsy stood there looking at him, trying to figure out what kind of game this was and when it was going to start, and the burglar looked back at him and as far around as he could without actually moving anything but his eyeballs. For all he knew this huge beast was ready to come right through the glass at him.

I went to the door and opened it. "You got five seconds to get out of this yard before I let him out."

He jumped the porch railing onto the flowerbed and went straight over the fence, ignoring the gate three feet away. I came back inside and told Mugsy he was a good boy.

That was a fine day; even better was the time some desperate junkie broke into Stan's apartment looking for drugs only to find Stan coming out of the shower. Stan chased him down the stairs and into the yard and he made an Olympian leap over the side fence into our yard, where he was safe from Stan but not from Rip and Mugsy. Rip took after him with Mugsy right behind barking happily. The thief barely touched the ground as he sprinted for the fence on the far side of our property. Over it he went, and then screamed from the depths of his soul. The girls who rented the house next door on that side belonged to an animal rescue society and always had dogs in their backyard waiting for adoption. Currently they had among their orphans several abused pitbulls and our fugitive must have seen them just as he vaulted over the fence. He pumped his legs like Wile E. Coyote attempting to run on air after going over the cliff and made it though their yard and over the back fence into the alley with surprising agility and speed. He, too, never returned.

It wasn't long before we were asking ourselves how we had ever struggled along with only one large dog. Despite his size Mugs deferred completely to Rip and Rip looked after him like some beloved but slightly unbright child. They had their own bowls on separate sides of the kitchen and developed a ritual where each would eat about half of his food after we set it down, and then race for the other bowl to make sure it was the same thing and not something better, then back again when they had finished licking them clean, just in case the other had neglected to eat all his food. It happened with such synchronization and reliability that Lynda began calling out "Change!" just before they did it, impressing many a guest who wondered just how (and why) we'd taught them this trick.

He was easy to love, but a problem child to raise. For all their size and strength Rottweilers are timid in many regards and fragile emotionally. Mugsy shrank and cowered from any raised voice and desperately wanted to please but had no idea of how to do it. He'd been locked up in solitary in the tiny basement apartment next door when he wasn't chained to the tree and Christ knows what they'd done to him wherever he'd been stolen from. His toilet training was nonexistent. He just did it wherever he was and cringed, waiting to be hit. We tried and tried to teach him to go to the door when he wanted out but he couldn't quite grasp the idea.

One morning Lynda went into the bathroom without locking the door. While she sat there, Mugsy poked it open with his nose and followed her in. He looked at her for a few moments then hunkered down beside her and peed all over the floor, a proud look on his face. Lynda could only pat his head and say, "Nice try."

We resorted to leaving spare towels everywhere so we could mop up his accidents. You couldn't paper train a dog like Mugs unless you got the Sunday *New York Times* seven days a week. You needed a big, thick beach towel, at the least, maybe a sleeping bag. Worse was when he squatted and dropped several pounds of steaming dog manure onto the floor, all the while staring at you with those huge, confused eyes. Poor, sweet Mugs—he held it until he was fit to burst and then let go, knowing it was wrong but out of options, at the mercy of colonic pressure.

It fell to me to clean it up; Lynda's stomach couldn't handle it and when she tried she gagged and convulsed and vomited, which only compounded the problem. Even a childhood on the farm mucking out stalls hadn't prepared me for this. I swaddled my hands with great fistfuls of paper towels and dumped it into grocery store bags, being careful to breathe only through my mouth; when I was a nightshift police reporter a cop taught me to do this at crime scenes with well-ripened dead bodies. It worked a treat with decomposing corpses but it didn't help at all with Mugs and

Lynda's mess. I finally just held my breath and dove in, trying to clean it up before I asphyxiated. Better that than death by toxic dog poop.

It was Rip who finally trained him. He followed Rip everywhere—up the stairs and back down, outside and around to the front, back down the walk and into the garden—and he faithfully followed Rip to the door and went out with him when he peed. Then one day he scratched at the back door by himself and we leaped up to praise and pet him, scaring the hell out of him with our enthusiasm.

When he shadowed him a little too close Rip turned and snapped at him half-heartedly and Mugs jumped back, but not for long. Where Rip went, Mugs followed as reliably as Monday follows Sunday. One day Lynda and I went out in the morning and with one thing or another came back late in the afternoon. One of us had forgotten to latch the gate when we went out; we could see it hanging open as we came down the alley, hearts sick with the thought of them out on the busy street or lost somewhere blocks away. But there they were a few houses down, grazing peacefully, Rip investigating something in the grass beside a garage and Mugs right behind him, like George and Lenny on a country road—*Where are we going, Rip? Are we going to see the rabbits?*

If we went out both dogs had to come in the Jeep, which about filled the cargo area. We became adept at packing around them when we bought plants and shrubs and bags of dirt for the garden, palm tree fronds and bamboo stakes poking out the back window and a dog hanging out either side. Both of them insisted on inspecting every shopping bag that came into the car or house, each one set down in front of them so they could jam their noses to the bottom and see what was what. They never took anything, just gave it the once-over and waved us through, like border guards in a good mood.

When we barbecued hamburgers we cooked a few for them, too, and couldn't imagine why anyone wouldn't. They lay on the kitchen floor while we ate, patiently waiting for us to put the leftovers down for them, and then toddled ahead of us up the stairs at bedtime.

Somehow we all fit on the queen-sized bed. When we renovated the attic bedroom Lynda and I had to camp out in the living room downstairs for several weeks. The mattress in front of the fireplace became our life raft and the dogs were sharks attacking on all sides. Our only hope was to feed them peanuts and popcorn and lure them up on the bed to watch TV with us.

At Christmas they had their own stockings and presents and had just as much fun tearing up the wrapping paper and ribbon as they did playing with the balls and rawhide chewbones inside. Bumstead, the elderly black-and-white cat, ignored them for the most part and slept under the cast iron radiators, keeping tabs with one lazy eye. When he did come out he often curled up with Rip and spent hours determinedly washing his head with his rough tongue, until we were sure he would leave a bald spot, Rip submitting to it with the same look on his face as a small boy having his cheek cleaned with an auntie's wet Kleenex.

Mugsy kept growing until he was more than twice Rip's size and we wondered if he would ever stop. His head came up to Lynda's waist and when he stretched out beside her on the bed, he was as long as she was and outweighed her by nearly half-again.

Mugsy was in fact more Ferdinand the Bull than cow. People would hurriedly lock their cars and run for their houses if they didn't know him, as this huge animal clomped sedately down the sidewalk toward them. They placed no faith in the dollar-store chain I was holding. While they rattled their keys trying to get safely inside, Mugs stopped and smelled the flowers or inspected a bee on a dandelion. Children were too fascinated to be afraid of him and he would stand patiently while a crowd of them patted and stroked and goggled at him. He was the biggest thing they'd seen outside of a zoo. When we barbecued in our backyard the neighbour kids would line up in our yard for rides and I'd lift them onto his back while Lynda led him around the house and back with a hamburger held out as enticement. When he got back to the starting line we gave him the burger and loaded a new kid or two on for the next trip. Rip would accept a hamburger but had no patience for playing pony. He laid down by the cooler and kept watch over the beer.

They were very different, Mugs and Rip. Mugs

never did adopt Rip's zero-tolerance policy towards strangers, though he barked in support when Rip warned one off through the gate. But he really thought of it more as a game than a call to arms. A stranger was just a friend he hadn't met, possibly one with sandwiches. And Mugs was never really one for running and leaping. Maybe it was his fractured childhood and the fact that no one had ever played with him but he was utterly baffled by the idea of chase-the-stick or get-the-ball. You threw it and waved your arms in encouragement and he just stood there looking at you as if to say, *Nice throw!—now what?*

He preferred a calm and careful pace when walking, with plenty of time to look around to enjoy the scenery. Cats on the porches and back fences stared at him with that false calm an anxious cat has, and he just looked back and moved on. By the time he was full-grown the cats who recognized him would saunter across the alley with only the merest glance at Mugs, a cursory nod and then back to their own business. If Rip was with us they stayed well up off the ground, tails twitching, and never took their eyes off him until we were out of sight.

The worst thing Mugs ever did in his entire life was one spring afternoon when he walked down the side of the house to the basement suite where the tenant woman had just fried up a steak for dinner. All that cooking must have tired her out because she put it down on the end table under the open window and then fell asleep on the couch. When Mugs wandered by he just stretched his neck through the window and helped himself, and she woke up with shreds of beef and dog slobber dripping down onto her face. She was so angry it looked like her head might explode and even though it didn't, the whole thing was very satisfying.

After Rip was gone, Scruff simply assumed the role of alpha dog, even though he was small and white and it was impossible to mistake him for anything but a cat. But Mugs deferred to him as well and Scruff accepted it as his due. Many times we saw Scruff walk up to where he was laying on the floor and stand there expectantly until Mugs vacated it. Then Scruff would turn around several times and lay down in the warm spot. Or simply push his way between Mug's enormous paws and curl up against his chest.

Scruffy also followed me whenever I went to the corner store, a white blur bounding behind hedges and up across the fences and it was hard to tell whether he was accompanying or stalking me. Once he waited for me at the end of the alley and when I came out of the store he was accepting worship from a little girl of six or so, arching his back and doing turnabouts as she stroked him. "Is he your cat?" she asked.

"He is," I said, and then added, "He likes to eat popcorn." It was completely true—Scruff would lay on the bed and wait to be fed if we were watching a movie and when we weren't quick enough his little white paw would slowly snake out and flick a few out of the bowl. He preferred to be served but in a pinch, he would get his own.

The little girl looked back at me with an expression of sadness and dismissal. "All cats eat popcorn. Everyone knows that." Self-esteem considerably deflated, I walked the rest of the way home alone. Scruff stayed awhile longer with her, pleased to be in the company of someone who knew cats so much better than I did.

*Chapter Seven*

# Rip, R.I.P.

*Well I had an old dog and his name was Blue*
*Bet you five dollars he's a good dog too*
*Bye bye Blue, you good dog you*
— OLD MOUNTAIN SONG

Dogs live a life unburdened by taxes but there's no escaping the other inevitability. The black camel eventually kneels at all tents, man and dog alike, and he came
for Rip roughly sixteen years after our friend brought
him home tucked inside her coat.

They had been fine years but they'd about worn
my dog out. He could no longer make it up onto the
bed and it hurt him too much for me to lift him. We
crushed up his arthritis pills and mixed them in with
his food but there were days when he simply couldn't
get up from where he lay; his back legs and hip joints
were just too stiff. We put hot-water bottles and finally an electric blanket on his hindquarters to help
get him moving again. I would lie down on the floor
with him and talk to him and pet him and he would

pant and look at me with those eyes filled with love and complete bafflement at what was happening to him. He seemed to be saying, "I don't know what's wrong but just give me a minute and we'll get up and at 'em."

Then he would try to get up and *ki-yi* pitifully until he finally got to his feet, wobbly but still game. Once up he was mostly the dog I had known for so long but only if I didn't look closely. His eyes were cloudy and his coat was worn out and balding in spots. Like the Velveteen Rabbit, he had been loved to pieces.

It was horrible to hear him suffer while trying to get up in the morning and every time he did, I breathed a sigh of relief, all the while knowing I would not be able to avoid the issue much longer. I knew exactly what Lynda meant when she said, "Sometimes I listen to him sleeping and I pray that he just stops breathing." We all wish that for the people we love, that they just fade away while dreaming of chasing rabbits or whatever gives them the most joy, but few of us get it and Rip was not one of them. He hung on and hung on until one day I finally made the appointment with Dr. Jim, our vet, to arrange the mercy killing of my best friend.

On the appointed day, we got up early and took Rip and Mugsy for their last walk together. Rip was fairly spry and I was very close to being convinced I should cancel, until we met another dog. In the introductions, as the three of them milled on the sidewalk, either Mugs or the other dog bumped Rip and he snarled.

I called him to me and saw that he was bleeding from one of his eyes. Just that incidental contact had split his skin open. He was really only hanging together out of habit.

We dawdled as much as we could but Rip was getting tired, still eager to go but walking stiff-legged on sore knees and hips. At the corner store I bought him an old favourite, a big can of Puritan beef stew. We gave it to him in his big silver dish and when he finished it I said "car ride" to him for the first time in several months and he came happily to the Jeep and barely yelped when I lifted him into the back.

He loved car rides. For the first few years I had him we didn't own a car. Then I found a job where I needed to drive and I took out a $3,500 bank loan for a '65 Mustang. Rip jumped in the first time I opened the door and held the bucket seat back for him, straight to the passenger side as if that had always been his spot. I remember driving somewhere and eating wine gums, peeling them out of the cellophane wrapper and reaching every second one back over my shoulder for Rip, one for him and one for me. He spat out the green ones if I gave him any—I didn't like them either.

He was still very excited to be back in the car, looking out the window on one side and then the other, though he had a hard time keeping his balance; rides had been few and far between lately. This was shaping up to be a pretty good day—a walk, beef stew, car trip. It was just getting better and better . . .

We were not as keen as he was.

It's odd how even at the most horrible times you can still think in terms of practicality. I parked the car as close to the door as I could because I knew I would have to carry him when we came back out. At the same time I was thinking this, and wondering where best to bury him in our yard, I was able to shut out what was happening and focus only on what I was doing right this instant: I wasn't taking Rip to the vet to be put to sleep, I was just driving down this street. I wasn't taking him for his last car ride, I was just turning left at the light. I was operating on two levels and the one where I was really conscious of what was going on was buried deep down, where you can think about the unthinkable, like your own death ticking closer every hour, in removed and pragmatic terms.

When I swung the back door open Rip was dancing on the floorboards, ready to go. He wanted to jump down and only a few years earlier he would have flown out of the back without a thought. Now he paced back and forth anxiously looking for an easier way down. Finally I put my hands on his sides and he jumped/ fell to the pavement. He would be sore later, but there wouldn't be a later so it didn't matter now.

Inside the vet's waiting room Rip was happy as could be. The assistant came over and fussed with him, turning her head away from him to quietly tell me that they would be ready for us in a minute, as if it were a secret we were keeping from him. Rip was more interested in the big cat in the carrying cage at the other end of the waiting room. I wonder if we would enjoy waiting rooms more if we had a better sense of smell and less idea what was coming.

Rip was too sore for me to lift up onto the vet's examination table so I spread his old blanket on the floor and lay down with him. The doctor gave him a quick looking over and said I was doing the right thing. I wanted to say that it may be right but it felt terribly wrong, but really, I could only go through with this if I worked very hard at not feeling anything. I felt very removed, as if it weren't really happening, though I had a stone the size of my heart in the middle of my chest. I rubbed his ears and whispered to him and he licked my face as the vet gave him the first needle, to put him to sleep, and then the second, final one. I kissed his muzzle and the vet said, "His heart's stopped." So had mine.

Lynda went out front to pay while I wrapped him in his blanket, picked him up, and took him out to the car. I was carrying sixteen years of my life when almost everything I did included this dog—a marriage, a honeymoon camping trip down the Pacific Coast, half a dozen homes, a divorce, some serious drinking after the marriage broke up and cab rides home from the bar to let Rip out and feed him while the cabbie waited. The night I came home and realized I had no dog food in the house so he got a frozen T-bone steak from the freezer.

I thought about the December night I was working evening shift and came home at two in the morning to find the furnace had died. There was ice in the toilet and a turtle I inherited after the breakup was frozen solid in his bowl. Rip and I slept on the kitchen floor under a dozen blankets, with the oven cranked up and its door open. The next day I took him to the newsroom with me and while I worked he lay under my desk, and on my lunch break I took him downstairs and he shat in the parking lot.

It took several days to get a repairman and we camped out in the kitchen, drinking beer and watching TV through the french doors to the living room. Churchy LaFemme, the turtle, made a complete recovery after I melted the ice with a hairdryer. A friend eventually took him and told me years later that as soon as he had a larger aquarium he began to grow and finished up the size of a small suitcase.

I remembered that Rip knew the ice cream man's song when we lived in the house just off Kingsway and when the driver turned down our street and he heard that Scott Joplin rag he would jump up and look at me expectantly. I was doing freelance writing then, and spent most of my time chained to the typewriter in the spare bedroom. Rip lay on my feet while I wrote so that he could sleep but be wakened immediately if I tried to go somewhere without him. Down the street we'd go with a handful of change and sit on the basketball court in the park while we ate our Fudgsicles. I held the stick for him and when he'd licked it clean, he chewed that up, too.

He played basketball on that court with me many times. He was a tenacious if unusually slobbery defensive player and rebounder, lunging and trapping the ball with his forepaws, snarling and barking and biting it. If you beat him off the dribble he didn't give up on the play, but ran between your legs and dumped you onto the tarmac. When he tried to trap the ball with his front paws he often hit it with his snout and pushed it away from him, so he'd end up chasing it across the court in a stop-and-start series of yips, leaps, and skittering bounces. He was, to be honest about it, a dirty player.

When we first moved into that house I was breaking up the cardboard boxes and burning them in the fireplace and Rip watched for a bit, then dove for a box, caught it in his paws and tore it to small pieces happily and with great pride of accomplishment. From then on I threw the boxes at him and he rendered them, growling and flinging the bits in the air, until there was nothing but a mound of pieces strewn across the floor like a giant's jigsaw puzzle. Then we sat down and fed them to the fire.

He could peel a mandarin orange, holding it in his paws and rotating it against his teeth, like an immense squirrel, until there was a single unbroken roll of peel left on the carpet. At Christmas if we left a bowl of oranges out he would finish the lot before morning and leave the peels scattered around. If we left a bowl of nuts out he would happily eat the whole thing, shells and meat, and leave shards everywhere for unsuspecting sleepy morning feet to discover. If we were awake, though, he would sit patiently while Lynda cracked the nuts open and fed him—one for Rip, one for Mugs, one for Lynda, and continue indefinitely, secure that she wouldn't have the heart to stop while they sat there, mouths open, as expectant as baby birds.

Rip liked a drink and he would take one if you offered it, or if you didn't. He used to knock drinks off the coffee table at parties so he could lap up the spillage, and he had a brief career as a rescue dog along the lines of the famous St. Bernards of the Alps, with casks of brandy affixed to their collars for reviving lost travellers. Instead of brandy Rip brought me cans of beer while I mowed the back lawn. Mary gave it to him in the kitchen and he would run down the back steps and across the grass to me. At least, he did for a while. Then on one trip his teeth punctured the cheap aluminum can and he got a mouthful of cold Rainier. Being sensible he laid down to enjoy it and the next time Mary gave him a can to ferry outside he just looked at her and bit down hard on it right there in the kitchen. We switched to bottles but he considered that to be petty on our part and flatly refused to carry them.

He hated hats, and uniforms. Police, postmen, deliverymen of all stripes, Salvation Army—it was all the same to him and I have no idea why, though the hat problem made more sense after I caught a man in a turban poking at him with an umbrella through the fence. When I caught him a second time I asked him if he would like me to let the dog out so he could play with him more easily but he declined and found a different route to use afterward. For the rest of his life Rip was strongly anti-hat. He never ran across a yarmulke but if he had he would have hated it, too. It would have been a mistake to take him to Nashville and he would surely have bit the living hell out of the Pope if he'd had a chance.

He was also willing to go after people wearing none of the above items. He responded to shouting and arguments by immediately joining in, barking and growling and changing sides at a whim. He was very sensitive to our moods. If we were angry so was he. He didn't need the details—he was in, on faith.

While we were living at the house off Kingsway my wife was sweeping up one morning and looked down the front steps to find a middle-aged man sitting in his car masturbating. She was out the gate in a flash, screaming and beating on the driver's side window with her broom while Rip attacked on the passenger side, paws on the door, barking his *I-want-to-eat-you-and-chew-the-bones* bark and trying to dig his way through the glass. The poor bastard fumbled to get his key in the ignition and screeched away from the curb, pants still at his knees, years of therapy looming.

I remembered that on a New Year's morning while we lived at that house we woke up still a little drunk from the night before, on a cold bright day that demanded we go up to Central Park with leftover champagne and Rip. We swigged wine while I threw the ball for him and when it rolled into the little creek he just charged in and stuck his head straight under to get it, up over his snout and muzzle, up to his eyes. Dogs aren't supposed to want to get their heads wet but he went full submersion, like a country Baptist. Just to be sure, I threw it in a few more times, and we shouted "Hallelujah!" and "Praise Be!" while he rooted and snapped and splashed and then brought the ball back to my feet. It was the closest to church I'd been in years. He was six then, only a little more than a third through his life.

It seemed a very long time ago. Now I lifted him out of the back of the Jeep and carried him past the garage gate down the side of the house to the front yard. He was much heavier now than he'd been before and it made me think of the term dead weight. It was an awkward chore made no easier by my crying. I stumbled a few times and finally put him down on the sidewalk near the front steps to the house.

We lived on a busy street with a twelve-foot cedar hedge out front and a six-foot fence behind it and on the sides. There were massive pines and cedars in the neighbouring yards so ours stayed very shaded and quiet despite the traffic. If you had to spend the rest of eternity in the ground it seemed like a nice enough place to do it. I picked a spot over by one corner and started to dig. Lynda stayed inside with Mugsy. We didn't want him to see the body.

It was tough going. Cedars send out a thick mat of tiny but very tough roots and they're hellish to try to break through. I moved a few feet over and tried again. It began to rain.

I went in the house and opened a beer then got back at it. It was useless. I couldn't get through the roots. I had another beer while I considered the problem, and another after that. I decided to bury Rip in one of the large flower beds instead. I got the hole dug and had some more beer. I was just tossing the empties on the lawn at this point. I couldn't stop crying—every time I stopped for a few minutes I would think about my dog and start up again.

I took several more breaks for beer and silent contemplation but finally the hole was deep enough and I bent down to pick Rip up for the last time. I was sobbing now, soaked by the rain and covered in mud. I knelt down to tuck the blanket around him and picked him up, then turned to place him in the grave and happened to look up at the neighbour's window, where the entire family of Asian immigrants who lived on the main floor were crowded around, all of them clearly aghast. I stared back and suddenly saw what they were seeing—an obviously disturbed man, filthy, hair in his face, surrounded by beer bottles, sobbing uncontrollably while he dug an unmistakeable hole with an equally unmistakeable shape wrapped in a shroud on the ground beside him. Rip was a big dog, and Lynda was a tiny woman. Bundled in a shroud, they looked about the same size.

The neighbours looked at me and I looked back at them and began laughing uncontrollably, which didn't really help matters. They left the window but I could still see them nervously peeping around the corner from time to time as I shovelled. I threw a can at the window. I think they were too afraid to call the police—I had room for plenty more holes in that yard.

When I was done I patted the soggy dirt down as best I could and placed a big rock at the head of the grave and wrote on it with a heavy felt marker:

*Rip—A Good Friend*

# Chapter Eight

# The Worst Dog in the World

We were down to one dog again and the house felt nearly empty without Rip, but not for long. Lynda was out in the far reaches of the Fraser Valley one afternoon visiting her mother when she called to say she'd seen a sign for Rottweiler pups pinned to a tree and she was going back to look at them on the way home. She called again a few hours later and said the situation was this—a couple living in a basement suite with two Rottis, male and female and neither of them fixed, had not surprisingly ended up with puppies, eight of them, and the landlord felt that ten dogs was an embarrassment of riches and requested that they bring the number back down or get out and take their mutts with them. They wanted a hundred dollars each. Should she buy one?

Of course she should, and a few hours later the Jeep pulled up and Lynda came through the garden gate carrying the smallest Rottweiler I had ever seen. It was the most I'd ever paid for a dog and the least amount of dog for the money I could imagine.

She set him down in a flower bed and he waddled into and over the plants, tripping at regular intervals, going face first into the dirt. Mugsy looked at him with concern. He was willing to be friends with anyone, but he really wanted to be assured that this was a dog first, or at least a very ugly and stupid cat.

He did not look like any kind of bargain and in a better world they would have paid us to take him. Lynda said the lady had taken her into the yard to a baby pen they were using as a kennel/nursery and, Lynda being Lynda, she just got in and sat right down to play with them. She was covered in baby Rotti's, like a live fur coat, trying to pick one and finally settling on "the feistiest one." She had plenty of time to regret that choice over the next few years.

He was a runt and as close to ugly as a puppy can get, with porcupine whiskers and a flat, squashed little snout like some type of hedgehog. On the way home she had him tucked in her jacket, which seems to be the accepted method of bringing kittens and puppies home, but on the freeway he bit and wriggled and finally squirmed free and fell headfirst into the gap between the driver's seat and the door, squealing pitiably while Lynda fished blindly with one hand for him, steering the car with the other. It took a while to pull him back out so he spent a fair bit of time with his head wedged in between the seatbelt mechanism and the door panel and she was convinced he was never quite right after that.

"I think I gave him brain damage," she said, as he

lurched and plopped through the garden, falling over his own feet and angrily biting the heads off flowers, emitting strange growls and yips for no discernible reason. She crouched down further to get a better look at him and he bit her soundly on the cheek, leaving pinprick toothmarks but not quite drawing blood. She screamed and he fell over, then bounced away looking for more trouble. It was the beginning of several years of hell. After he ate an entire bed of young hosta shoots, we named him Sluggo because until then we'd only had to protect the garden from slugs. He was the worst dog in the world.

As with Mugsy, we nearly despaired of ever housebreaking him and when we scolded him for going on the floor, he stood there on his fat little legs and looked back with complete impudence—Lynda described how the dog-mines and puddles on the floor were nothing compared to the anger she felt looking at "that insolent little face."

He didn't care that you were upset. If you picked him up and looked him in the eye and tried to get your point across he sneered and took a snap at your nose. The cat hated him and Mugs, who had the forbearance of all the assembled saints and Anne Sullivan . . . endured him.

He was still tiny, so small that when he went for his first walks with Mugs he couldn't quite get up over the curb when we crossed the street. He chewed the leash and ran under Mugsy's legs and bit his ankles, tying him up like a furry, spiked bolo. Mugs did what he always did when something unpleasant happened: he stood stock-still with a concerned expression on his face and waited for someone to make things right. In this case it meant weaving Sluggo back through and around Mug's legs, biting and snapping the whole way.

People would stop and say, "Oh, he's so cute" because even the ugliest pup is still adorable, and Sluggo was a ball of black and brown fur that looked like it had just detached itself from Mugsy and somehow come to life. There were days when we wanted to say, "Yes he is, you want him?" but we didn't because as much of a trial and a punishment for our sins as he was, we loved him.

Well, I loved him—Lynda was fond of him but never did quite trust him after she'd been bitten a few more times. I loved him even though he had done horrible things to me. He chewed the heel of a prized guitar. He shredded books left anywhere he could get to them. One night, through a fog of sleep, I heard him tumble off the bed and patter out to the hall where he whimpered and whined until I got up. He had thrown up several times earlier in the day with one of those dog illnesses where they simply expel everything in their system until they feel better. From the amount he'd unloaded we thought he was done.

Not even close. I got up in the dark and left the light off so as not to wake Lynda. The smell hit me as I stepped into the hall but too late to warn me; I stepped into a pool of sick-puppy diarrhea and performed a perfect, silent-film comedy pratfall onto my back. I was naked, cold, covered from hair to toenails in liquid dog crap and likely paralyzed, but the smell encouraged me greatly and I managed to get to my feet and into the bathtub to clean myself off. Lynda called from the other room and I was so angry that when I answered it was unrecognizable as English, or any other language. She did not enquire further and I finished the job in silence, then used the towels to clean the hallway floor. Sluggo had already wheedled Lynda into taking him back up onto the bed where he was curled up and dreaming, leaving me to drink middle-of-the-night beer and smoke at the kitchen table while I seriously questioned some of my life decisions.

Despite everything, he was my dog and if I didn't kill him then I certainly wasn't going to let anyone else do it. There's a theory that we mammals are genetically predisposed to respond sympathetically to babies; hawks eat the hatchlings from other bird's nest and baby sea turtlets are a beachside smorgasbord for any critter who comes along while they're making their way to the ocean. But not we warm-blooded types. And a good thing, else we would throw them all in the river.

Crying, biting, howling, defecating, vomiting—we just wipe them (and ourselves) off and tend to them, trying to remember what it was like to sleep for more than fifteen minutes at a stretch. In humans—and many animals; we've all seen things like the pig who suckled the orphaned kittens—that nurturing, parental feeling extends to all small, helpless furry things. Sluggo was a testament to all this and despite the provocation we simply put up with him and hoped one day for deliverance.

When he had grown slightly larger he developed the habit of biting onto Mugsy's tail and following behind him, like a baby elephant behind his mother. An evil baby elephant, possessed by demons. I remember Mugs coming around a corner with Sluggo fastened onto his rear and just standing there staring at me with a forlorn look on his face that said, "Please, help me." But there was nothing I could do. We were all in the same boat.

One morning I took both dogs out into the alley for a quick watering before I left for work. I was standing there with my coffee cup while Mugs sniffed at things and Sluggo yapped and snarled and roared back and forth among the garages and trashcans. Suddenly a large and surly shepherd-cross I'd never seen before came through a section of broken fencing and went for Mugsy's throat. His thick leather collar protected him but Mugs was about as likely to fight as he was to stand up on his back legs and sing Rossini's *Largo al Factotum*.

When the shepherd got nowhere tearing Mugsy's throat out, he wheeled and went after Sluggo. Apparently he'd been absent the day we covered the whole section on not eating babies. Sluggo squealed like a piglet and scurried across the lane. He was head-

ing for the fence but caught his shoulders between
two pickets and was too terrified to figure out how to
squeeze through so he just stuck there, legs churning
and pumping at full speed, throwing up dust and small
rocks, getting absolutely nowhere and digging a pair of
small trenches.

It all took place in seconds and without actually
thinking about it I launched myself at the attacker,
caught hold of his collar and punched him in the head
several times. One of the first things you learn as a dog
owner is never to stick your hand into the middle of a
dogfight, but reason and good judgement had fled in
the heat of battle.

This surprised the hell out of both of us and he
bucked like a wild horse, threw me off, and went after Mugs again. I grabbed the nearest thing to hand, a
metal garbage can, raised it up and smashed it across
his back with all my might. It made a terrible sound
and I think scared him more than it hurt but he'd had
enough anyway and ran off down the lane.

Mugsy was still trying to figure out what had happened and Sluggo was crying under the fence. My
hands were covered in scratches and gouges and dripping blood. I got the three of us back in the house and
settled down. Lynda had to hold Mugs and reassure
him that everything was okay now, but Sluggo was already over it, as if it had never happened. He was happily murdering a sock on the dining room floor.

When I got to work I was pouring a cup of coffee
when one of the other reporters, an older lady, asked

what on earth had happened to my hands. "Dogfight,"
I told her, without thinking. For the rest of my time
there she avoided me.

Not long afterwards I was trying to explain our
struggles with Sluggo to another writer at the paper,
Trevor Lautens, a wise and courtly man and an unre-
pentant dog lover. Trevor related how his own young
dog, Booker, had terrorized the cat, destroyed his
home, threatened his marriage, and ruined his nerves.
He concluded, "I know how you feel. I love that dog
but sometimes I wish I'd never seen his face." I knew
just what he meant. I was a prisoner of the Chinese
Obligation; I had taken Sluggo in and now I was responsible for him, so long as we both lived.

One afternoon he came into the kitchen walking at
a noticeable angle, about fifteen degrees to one side,
like a badly loaded freighter in a rough sea. He stag-
gered around, drank an entire bowl of water and fell
over. Oh Christ, he's been poisoned, I thought, and we
hustled him into the Jeep and down to the emergency
after-hours vet. He made it into the waiting room under his own power, still staggering and listing to port,
and the assistant took him into the back to draw some
blood.

About twenty minutes later the vet came out and
said, "Do you smoke pot?" I thought he was offering to
sort us out before giving the bad news and I was about
to ask if he had any brandy but then he said, "Because
your dog's going to be fine but he's stoned out of his
gourd."

The vet asked if maybe we'd left our stash out where Sluggo could have gotten into it. The old ladies in the waiting room with their arthritic cats and malignant canaries heard this and there was a chorus of *tsk*ing and muttering. What kind of monster would feed dangerous, illegal drugs to a poor little dog?

"No, we don't," I told him. I thought that was sufficient and really, there didn't seem to be any good way to tell him that of all the many drugs I'd done (most of them) I just never really enjoyed marijuana. I could imagine the rest of the waiting room crowd scrambling in their purses for heart pills if I did.

"Well, he got it somewhere," the vet said. He had the manner of a prosecuting attorney asking me how the bloody hammer just happened to be in my closet.

Then I had an idea. "What about the leaves and sticks from a marijuana plant? I'm always pulling him out of bags of garbage in the alley. Could he have eaten that?" The Eastside was filled with rental houses that had been converted to indoor marijuana farms and there were two or three we knew of in the neighbourhood. They weren't particularly hard to spot, tinfoil scotch-taped over the windows and a smell like they were breeding skunks inside.

"That would do it, sure. The trimmings from a plant still have a good amount of THC in them. He'll be fine, just let him have all the water he wants and he'll be okay in a day or so." He slept it off splayed out on the kitchen floor near his water dish and when he did come around he ate like a pair of draft horses.

By the time Sluggo was a year old he had filled out in all directions and effected a caterpillar-like transformation into a long-legged, handsome dog who looked nothing like the misfit Lynda had brought home.

He was still a terror, though. Even an expensive two-week stay at an obedience school couldn't straighten him out. When we picked him up after graduation they were happy to see the hind end of him and told us that they'd done their best but they made no promises. From this I had to conclude that the school embraced "social advancement" and similar types of enlightened, modern education — graduation didn't necessarily mean you'd learned anything, just that you had showed up more often than not and hadn't killed anyone.

They brought him out and made him sit. He did seem to be noticeably calmer and more attentive. He walked nicely to the car, on his leash, so long as you said "Heel!" every few feet. It wasn't much but we'd take it.

We stopped for lunch on the way home at an outdoor cafe and I slipped the handle of his leash under the heavy metal leg of the table and relaxed. He wasn't going anywhere now. "Stay," I told him in the firm voice the trainers had coached us in, giving the hand command, and he laid down obediently. A few minutes later I got up to go to the bathroom and Sluggo and the table followed me, leaving a trail of dishes, glasses, cutlery surprised diners and restaurant staff behind us on the patio. So much for obedience. I suggested we try the drill sergeants at Parris Island next; Lynda said we needed an exorcist.

But he really was better after training. We were not the best masters, anyway. My worst mistake was teaching Mugsy "Go." He would stop unfailingly at corners and wait for me to give him the word, and then he'd cross the street. It was one of his favourite things, twitching with anticipation until he heard the command and then coming out of the blocks. Mugs was built for comfort, not speed, but even so when he set out for the horizon, if you were at the other end of his leash you went with him. (It took me awhile to develop the reflexes to drop the leash when this happened; my right arm is now slightly longer than the left.)

Unsurprisingly, one of the words I used most often with Sluggo was "No!" When I had them both out and yelled at Sluggo to stop whatever he was doing, which happened several times per block, Mugsy thought he heard the starter's gun and took off. Sluggo bolted, too. Mugs was only good for half a block or less at a sprint and when he slowed down Sluggo nipped and barked and circled him, encouraging him to go again. It took me several minutes to get him calmed down enough to continue, and then it happened all over again.

Finally I hit on a system of pre-emptive exhaustion and took them both down the lane and across the street to a long alley with a downward slope. I threw Sluggo's hard rubber ball as far as I could and we watched him run at top speed until he was about the size of a squirrel, and then back up the hill at a full gallop, panting and dripping great ribbons of drool. After a dozen or so of these, he was manageable and we could have our walk. Mugsy waited patiently with me while Sluggo ran—for the first few tosses he would run ten feet or so, just out of good sportsmanship, but it was like entering a wooly mammoth in the Kentucky Derby. You might admire the effort but you wouldn't want to bet on him.

Mugsy did actually really run once, though he never had any interest in chasing balls or sticks. He would ather stay close by us when we went out. But one nice afternoon we walked up to the nearby school and he got interested in something or other and dawdled while we continued around the corner and up the next street. When he looked up, we were most of a block away and he didn't like it at all.

We called him and he took off like he'd been drop-kicked by god. Around the corner he came, past the high, chain-link fence of the baseball diamond, flat-out and bent sidewise into the turn like a champion race-horse, legs flashing in that strange configuration where the front pair are stretched back in unison and the back ones are forward, and all of them off the ground at the same time. He was going so fast he ran right past us and all the way to the end of the block before he could stop without falling over, and he stood there waiting for us to catch up. By the time we got home he was limping.

Over the next while his limp got a little worse, then a little better, then worse again and finally bad enough that we took him to our vet. Dr. Jim felt along his leg and knees and between us we managed to get him in position for X-rays. When the pictures came back Jim said, "He's torn his anterior cruciate ligament but we can fix it with nylon line, very strong stuff. It's what they use to fish for tuna."

Lynda remembers him saying the operation was very common now and that Harrison Ford had just had it. I remember it being George Clooney but either way it had a movie star price tag—three thousand dollars. He was on his way back to being a five-thousand-dollar Rottweiler again.

# Chapter Nine

# The Death of Mugsy

Mugs came home from the vet with half his leg shaved bare and a frightening incision down the side, edges stitched together with heavy black thread of the kind you'd imagine using to sew up canvas sails for a whaling vessel. The wound oozed and dripped and we took turns bathing it with clean water and antiseptic and trying to keep him on the bed we'd made him beside our own. This wasn't easy because he wanted to be up on ours with us, not down on the floor. He was a gentle soul but he was also more than 150 pounds of very determined dog. Eventually we rigged steps out of a suitcase and a trunk and he clambered up them onto a quilt we sacrificed to the cause.

He spent most of his convalescence on the bed, lying back on pillows, watching gardening shows and cartoons and being petted and scratched. Getting back down was harder and it took Lynda and I on both sides to reassure him. He descended from the bed with the same caution and lack of enthusiasm as an elderly man getting into a rowboat. Once he was down he was very pleased with himself and couldn't wait to get back up.

We didn't have any way to get him into the back of the Jeep short of an engine hoist but I had an old Mustang and Lynda took him for rides around the neighbourhood in that. People stopped on the sidewalks and stared at this huge black shape sitting in the backseat with his great head scraping the roof, taking in the sights. Mugsy smiled back with his huge white teeth gleaming. He looked like Idi Amin reviewing the troops.

Before long he was completely healed and stood there patiently while I cut and pulled the sutures out. His knee seemed fine but now we noticed he'd begun to limp on the other leg. We took him back to Doc Dodds and he said it was likely Mugs strained it over-compensating for the weakness in the injured leg, and it had probably also hurried along an incipient hip problem, something Rottis are prone to.

It was the beginning of the end for Mugs. He was less able to walk and play and he put on weight because of it, and the weight compounded the hip problem and the sore hip made it harder to exercise and keep his weight down.

He had always been big but now he became huge. He reminded me of old basketball players like Moses Malone or Kevin Willis, big, big men even in their playing days but once they retired and began to put on pounds they became simply immense. I once saw Willis on a talk show some years after his playing days were done, wearing a tan corduroy suit. He looked like a sofa with eyes.

But Mugs was happy even if he limped. He liked to lay on the back porch with his rear end up on the hot deck and his front paws straight out and resting several steps down. He was a noble looking dog at any time but in this pose he looked like a great obsidian sphinx. From this vantage point he could survey his lands and when necessary bark at anyone coming down the lane with a distinct and very convincing *don't-make-me-come-down-there* tone. If he stayed home when we went out he barked in joy from his perch when we returned, his stump of a tail furiously shaking, and we'd stop on the stairs to let him stick his head in every shopping bag as if he were some giant, hairy customs agent. He was growing old before his time but we lied to ourselves that he still had many good years left. In our hearts we knew he didn't.

It wasn't long before he spent most of his time lying down. He whimpered when we left the room because he so badly wanted to be with us, but that meant trying to get up again. It wasn't long until it took all morning for him to get down the steps to the garden and all afternoon to climb back up to the porch, like Oscar Wilde struggling all morning to take out a comma and all afternoon to put it back in.

Lynda said that from the waist up he was the happiest dog in the world. We wondered, not entirely joking, if we should get his hind end removed and just have wheels attached. "Dumb old legs," Lynda said, massaging his hips. He stared up at us with such love and gratitude we would have to switch places so the other one could go cry where he wouldn't see.

Rottweilers are astoundingly stoic animals and can stand a terrible amount of pain without showing any indication of it. When Mugs was only a couple of years old we went to visit Lynda's father in Victoria. He had a beautiful house on a saltwater bay and we were sitting in the hot tub drinking wine around midnight while Mugs ran back and forth at the water's edge, annoying ducks and gulls and daring the harbour seals to come up on dry land. As we were drying ourselves off to go inside we called him. He came up the long yard like a rocket, straight past us and into the kitchen through the glass sliding doors, which were unfortunately closed at the time. They exploded inward as if we were being shelled from offshore.

Once through, while glass was still tinkling down, he stood stock-still, in shock. When we got to him, wrapped in towels and picking our way in bare feet, we saw that his face had been sliced open so that his lips now opened vertically as well as horizontally, hanging down in quadrants and pouring blood. He looked like something from a science fiction movie and it was all I could do to stanch the blood with a towel. Lynda could barely look at all.

We wrapped ice in fresh towels and held them to his face and through it all he stood there without a sound, just a sorrowful look in his eyes. I made a pathetic attempt to put a butterfly bandage on the wounds but it fell off immediately and Mugs spent the night licking his lips and face endlessly while we waited for the vet to open his office. When he did Mugs happily jumped into the Jeep and back out of it into the surgery, where Lynda held him and the doctor sewed him up. You would have thought he was having his toenails painted for all he cared, except that he would have shown more interest in that than he did in the stitching.

"They don't feel pain like we do—they just ignore it," the vet said. "I had a dog in here who stuck his face in a boat propeller while they were working on it in a garage. Awful mess, like hamburger, but he just sat there while I worked on him."

Mugs acted as stoic as Marcus Aurelius but we knew it had to be excruciating if he was crying. We tried every painkiller the vet would give us—finally in desperation I called my friend Jimmy, whose father was a lifelong racetrack trainer. The next day Jimmy brought over a small jar of powder and a note from his dad that read, "I use 2 tablespoons of this mixed into peanut butter for a 2,000 pound mare so for a 170-pound dog . . . goddamned if I know. Good luck. —George"

By now, Mugs spent almost all his time on the floor by Lynda's side of the bed, holding court from his nest of blankets like a dowager empress, swaddled from the waist down but head erect and alert. When he whined to go outside I would drag him down the hall to the front door on his blankets, like a frontiersman hauling his injured partner in a travois. It was backbreaking to do and upset Mugs; he was happy to be outside when he got there but the idea that you could keep moving after you lay down was deeply troubling to him.

I loved him with all my heart and he loved me, but he was Lynda's dog and as bad as I felt for Mugs and myself, I was more worried about how Lynda would take what I knew was coming. I feared that when the terrible day came I would have a dead dog and a wife with a nervous breakdown.

I worried about Sluggo, too. He saw Mugs as more than an older brother. He worshipped him, and now that he was two he'd been mimicking Mugs for so long he'd become a good dog. No, that's a lie; he was less awful than he'd been but still not really what you could call good. He came when you called, if he felt like it, as opposed to not at all, which was how he used to respond. He still wouldn't stay in the back of the Jeep and I spent every trip with him with my arm stretched between the seats, holding him back. He had a dozen other bad habits and general failures of behaviour but we were used to him now, the way you get used to certain relatives.

The horse medicine was just a last-ditch effort to buy Mugsy—us—a little more time but he was in bad way. It was so hard for him to get up. We tried to encourage him to just pee where he was and we would mop it up, but the dog who wouldn't be house-trained couldn't do it, and he held on until he could stand it no longer. Then he struggled to his feet with horrible moans and out onto the porch, squatting like a girl dog because he couldn't lift his legs any longer. Once he was back on his mat, though, he was all smiles and we brought his food bowl and water dish in so he could reach them without moving.

The horse medicine was in an old jam jar and there was no writing on it, so we studied the note and made our best guess at a dosage. Then we added a touch more and mixed it into some canned dog food. Mugs licked it up off a big wooden spoon and we waited. He looked back at us for a moment and suddenly sat up straight, more spry than he'd been in weeks, raring to go. Then his eyes rolled back and he fell like a tree into a French door, busting out several panes as he went down.

We thought we'd killed our dog and looked at each other in horror, then he began to snore at a volume that threatened the rest of the glass in the house. It was probably the first real rest he'd had for a long time and I think that's when we knew it was time to make arrangements.

Death is the subject of much intellectual and spiritual examination but it also carries practical, mundane considerations; what suit should Uncle Frank be buried in and what should we do with the rest of his clothes, who's going to call his bank and his credit card company and cancel the cable and go through his bills, can we keep cousin Brian away from the bottle at the wake. In our case it was the practical issue of what to do after we did what we had to.

Lynda and I had decided the vet needed to make a house call. Mugs was too big to carry and hurting too bad to walk, even to the car. I suppose we might have rigged up a ramp so he could get into the Jeep, but it seemed, too, that he should die at home surrounded by all of us, with the least amount of upset and fuss we could manage for him. It's what we would want, and it was what we wanted for him.

The vet put us in contact with a removal service that would come to the house and take away his body for cremation; there was no way I could dig a hole big enough to bury him on our property, and no way to get him into it if I did. He was twice Rip's size and after that experience I didn't think I had it in me to bury another loved one country-style. By the time I was done with Rip's funeral I was so physically and emotionally exhausted I just wanted to crawl in beside him and have Lynda kick some dirt over us.

On the last day of Mugsy's life the sun came up and shone brightly through the bedroom windows. Lynda was holding together well, which only made me fear what would happen when she couldn't any longer. Mugsy was more than just a special dog, he was an amalgamation of favoured child, beloved protector, best friend, co-pilot, and soulmate. I knew I would need to be strong; Lynda was going to need me when she finally crumbled.

The vet came and made his preparations while we waited for the removal service to show up. We'd scheduled them together so that we could move Mugs immediately. When the removal company's men arrived they turned out to be Sandra, a young woman about five-foot-four and 120 pounds. I had been expecting bruisers, big husky types along the lines of the Beagle Boys from Donald Duck or the lumpy, thick-necked bald guy in the heavy grey sweatsuit who always played the masseuse in old movies. Instead they sent me one of Santa's elves.

As we came down the hall and into the back bedroom she told me not to worry, she was much stronger than she looked and did this work all the time. Her voice trailed off as she caught sight of Mugs and I heard her mutter an involuntary *Jesus Christ* as she took in his size. The vet had given Mugs a painkiller and a sedative so he wouldn't be spooked by the commotion and he was licking Lynda's face and hands while she petted him and talked into his ear.

"What a shame," the vet said as he readied the next needle. "Such a beautiful, happy animal." Then, "I'm ready whenever you are. Do you need a few minutes?"

"No," Lynda said. "He's happy and he's not in pain. I don't want him to start hurting again. I want this to be the last thing he remembers."

Sluggo and Scruff were banished to the hallway but snuck around and watched through the French doors in my office. I got down beside him on the floor and put my arms around his neck, trying to hold the tears back until it was over.

"I love you, Mugs. I'm so sorry," I said. I could feel his warmth and his big heart beating against me. Then he gave a deep sigh and relaxed, as if he had been carry-ing a great load and had finally put it down. I knew he was gone, and that's when I fell apart. I let out a moan so loud and from so deep inside me that it took a sec-ond to register that it was me who'd made it. I began to heave with wracking sobs and couldn't stop. I clung to his neck and wept so hard I couldn't draw enough breath.

Lynda put her arms around me and held me. I hadn't cried like this since I was a child and maybe not even then. I heard the vet say, "This is the hardest part of the job. I can't take seeing this." By the time I could control myself, he was gone. Sandra was wait-ing outside the door and I asked her to come in. I was still wiping snot onto my sleeve. Lynda was completely calm.

"How do you want to do this?" I asked, and realized as I said it that she had no idea. I'd told the lady on the phone when we booked the appointment that we had "a very large dog."

"Right, large dog," she answered, typing away at her keyboard. "That's two hundred and twenty-five dollars plus taxes."

"This is a very large dog, an exceptionally large dog. He weighs—"

"Anything over a hundred pounds is a large dog. Do you want to arrange for cremation?"

So here we were; Sandra had a wicker basket in her van, which would be fine if you had a large load of laun-dry. What we had was more like the corpse of Babe the

Blue Ox. We might have to roll him on logs, the way lumberjacks hauled timber down a skid road.

"Could we wrap him in that big quilt and then carry it like a sling?" she asked. Sure, I thought—and maybe I could pick myself up by the hair, hold myself out at arm's length and let the leprechauns run wires from my toes to my forehead so they could play me like a harp.

We arranged him on the quilt and pulled at the corners until we had them twisted up into handles and slid him down the hall and through the kitchen, the same way I'd shuttled him out to pee so many times in the last few weeks. We got him onto the porch and out to the top of the stairs and then stopped, gasping. There were about a dozen steps down.

Lynda was holding Sluggo's collar and Scruff was running along the overhead lattice of the porch, peering over the edge. They were both very concerned with what was going on. Scruffy had been sleeping with Mugs most of the time, curled up beside him or in between his giant paws, tucked under his chin. He regarded Mugsy as his dog and always had.

"Ready?" I said, and hoisted my side of the bundle. Sandra took the first step and then another and I lunged to keep up. She took two more in a clumsy hop and then lost her grip and Mugs rolled out of the blanket onto the steps. I was furious. Sluggo got away from Lynda and ran past me down the steps to Mugs.

"Let him see so he understands," Lynda said, and

sure enough Sluggo gave a few troubled sniffs and then went back up the stairs to Lynda's side.

I wrestled Mugs back into the quilt and we hoisted him again. By the time we got him to the van and into the back, I was pouring sweat and bent over like I'd been doing stoop labour for forty years. How she got him out at the end of the ride was her business.

A few minutes later we stood on the back porch with a drink and contemplated struggling through life with only one dog. Scruffy was lying across the edge of the porch with his tail hanging down and twitching. Sluggo was lying quietly at the top step. Everyone was calm. I was a mess.

"I thought I was going to have to take you to the hospital by the time this was over," I told Lynda. "How did you do it?"

"I said goodbye to him when I saw how much pain he was in. It was my job to help him and that's what I did. He doesn't hurt anymore. That's all that matters." She was a tough customer. A week or so later we picked up Mugsy's ashes and planted them under a palm tree in the garden.

# Chapter Ten

# Friendly Isn't the Word for It

A few years after Mugsy died we sold the house on East 12th Avenue and moved downtown. In the dozen years we'd been there Mt. Pleasant had improved greatly. Young families had flocked there for the same reason we did, because it was one of the few areas in Vancouver where people of moderate income could afford to buy a house. Consquently prices went up and it was suddenly a good time to sell.

About the same time I took a buyout from the newspaper and opened a recording studio in the Downtown Eastside, so we looked for a house to buy, too. Lynda was dubious about the area but I've always felt a strange connection to it. When I was growing up it was where my Dad and my Uncle Mac drank, and when I was a few years older and moved to Vancouver myself it was where I lived and where my band rehearsed. This, though, was before the days of crack and meth and before the mass closure of the long-term mental hospitals.

The DTES was merely picturesque in the late seventies in comparison to the war zone it is today. The homeless and the abandoned insane roam the streets and alleys, dealers and hookers do business on the sidewalk in plain sight and the junkies fix there, too. I've seen people smoking crack outside the central cop shop, the Public Safety Building on Main Street, while cops hurried past them. It's a place that teaches you that "normal" and "acceptable" are relative terms.

One afternoon Lynda, a neighbour and I watched a transgender woman, either on drugs or not on enough of them, stand in the middle of the street shouting inarticulate abuse and waggling her penis at the passing cars. We called the police and told them what was happening. They said, "Well, he hasn't really done anything. Call us if he does."

My neighbour said, "Well, at least we know where the line is. You can stand in the road and shake your dick at strangers."

It's a grim place but not without its charm, and like all undervalued neighbourhoods it attracted artists, poets, and musicians, because it was what they could afford. We used the money from the house we sold to buy a "distressed property," two ancient houses on a single lot three blocks from the recording studio. On one corner was the Union Gospel Mission, on the other was the Downtown Mental Health Unit and between them we had the bases covered; if psychotherapy and drugs failed, there was always Jesus. The first of the two houses was a small two-storey built in the back of the property sometime in 1896 according to the city's water service records. The larger house in front went up a dozen years later. They were built by a sea captain named MacDonald who no doubt chose the location for its short walk to the docks. In their century-long existence his houses had been flophouses, crack dens, whorehouses, and every other kind of shady usage imaginable.

Shortly after we moved in we had a visit from two plainclothes cops from the homicide department who said they wanted to take some line-of-sight measurements in the back house to verify testimony in a murder trial. "No one told you about this when you bought the place?" one said as he tied a string to the bannister of the staircase. He handed the other end to his partner, who reeled it out into the living room and stood in different spots on our carpet while the first sighted down it.

"Well, here's what happened." He crouched down and took another look as his partner moved a few feet over at the far end of the line. "There were these two Vietnamese drug dealers and they brought a prostitute home to have some fun with. They're getting all lit up and having a fine old time when the two guys need to go upstairs for something. When they come back down they see the girl going through their jackets, stealing dope. So they killed her and chopped up the body and put it in garbage bags and dumped them a few blocks away in a garbage bin." His partner wrote down measurements in a little notebook.

"So after we get them, which wasn't too hard, the

one of them says 'Oh no, I never killed anybody—it
was my buddy. I came down the stairs and saw him doing it.' So now we have to measure from where he says
he was standing to where he says he saw this crime, to
see if it adds up, then we go back and tell the Crown
counsel if he's a reliable witness." His partner sniggered
at this and wrote something else down. They had a cup
of coffee and thanked us for our time. We never heard
any more about it but one Rottweiler hardly seemed
sufficient.

Before we could move in the places needed major
repair. The first step was hauling out almost three
tons of garbage: broken chairs, stained and torn mat-
tresses, piles of clothing, suitcases we were afraid to
open. We wore gloves with steel mesh liners because
of the hundreds of used needles strewn throughout the
place—one sink was unusable and when we wrenched
open the rusty P-trap it was completely clogged with
them, a literal stack of needles. In one backpack we
found a massive jar filled with pills, homemade by the
look of it, as the gel-caps had no markings at all. My
old friend Bill was acting as contractor for the reno
and we looked at the pills and then at each other. Once
upon a time we would have tried a couple of them, just
out of scientific curiosity. We tossed them with the rest
of the debris and had a beer instead.

The job took most of a month and once it was safe
I brought Sluggo down with me every day. There
were still more than a hundred years of smells accu-
mulated in the houses and he investigated every one

of them. There was one closet he poked his nose into and growled at, backing away as he did, then carefully ignoring it afterwards. I was just as happy he couldn't tell me what he suspected.

Dogs on construction sites are a hazard; they want to help and they're convinced you'll botch the job if they aren't allowed to supervise. But Sluggo was less dangerous than most when it came to getting underfoot and there was no keeping him out of things anyway.

Early on when there were several power saws in use in the courtyard I locked Sluggo in the main house and went to haul some boards. When I got back he was running around the courtyard "helping." I told everyone, again, that he needed to be kept away from the power tools or he'd stick his face in one, and locked him back up in the house.

Five minutes later Sluggo stuck his nose into my face while I was bent over to lift something. I cursed everybody and was cursed back in turn; they all swore no one had let him out. So I locked him back in the main house and before I could walk away Bill called me back.

The knob was turning by itself, like in a horror movie. It turned a bit, then stopped, then turned some more and finally clicked open and here came Sluggo. I put my hand on the inside knob and it was covered in slobber. It was a fine trick but expensive. Work stopped for almost an hour as everyone crowded around to watch the dog open a locked door. I should have sold hot dogs and beer. By canine standards Sluggo was a genius, but a serious underachiever.

On the job he stuck by my side no matter where I went, for as long as he could stand it. Then he raced off and inspected every room in both houses to make sure things were progressing according to his high standards. By the time the crew gathered in the kitchen of the big house every night to have a few quitting-time beers he was exhausted but every morning when Bill picked me up at seven a.m. Sluggo was ready to get back to it, more so than we were. He leaped into the back of the truck, full of plans for the day.

He was a dedicated foreman—no job was too small for him to give it a thorough going over, whether it was a hole we cut in the top floor to get at some leaking pipes, but which Sluggo believed was made so that he could get a better vantage point for overseeing work in the kitchen below, or a tiny spider-infested crawlspace running along one side of the foundation. Once the rotting wood door had been pried off he was in there several times a day. We could hear him digging and whining but he never got whatever he was after, for which we were all a little grateful. I had no interest in a return visit by the homicide bulls.

Maybe it was simply growing up or the weight of his many responsibilities on the job site but something very strange happened: Sluggo became a Good Dog. I loved him despite his many failings—his chewing, his biting, his failure to obey commands except on the rare occasions when he just felt like it for no damn reason at all. But as the summer wore on and we were close to moving in, I realized that Sluggo had changed.

Maybe it's like the person at work who loses a lot of weight. You see them every day and don't really notice, then one day you look and go, "Holy shit, where did Bob go?" Maybe Sluggo did that, getting a little better every day until I finally noticed. Maybe it was the responsibility of running a renovation crew. Or maybe, as I suspect in my heart, he just wanted to fuck with me.

Or it could have been that just as a man is never really an adult until his father dies, Mugsy's death gave Sluggo room to become The Dog, a heavy set of responsibilities and one that will age you quickly, like the presidency.

It may also have been the high regard he was held in by our neighbours. When I went up to the little store on Hastings Street he always came with me and we developed a system. I should say, he did. I hooked his leash to his collar and then he took the leash in his mouth and trotted about ten feet in front of me, turning his head every few seconds to look back over his shoulder with that sweet, intelligent face and verify that I was still coming right behind him. Then he went a little further. And did it again. For some reason he was concerned that I might wander off on my own, and then what would happen to me? He stood by my side at the lights and waited, then took the point again.

He needed the lead time to stop and be fussed over. He always stopped at the 20-Hour Market, a little grocery whose name was perfectly appropriate. It closed for four hours a day and never the same ones two days running so that if you saw it open you bought what you needed now, not later. There was no telling when or why he would put the steel gates down and disappear. He waited for a customer to go in or out and when they did he stuck his head through. The owner would cry, "Sluggo, my friend!" and feed him licorice and ice cream bars.

The girls working the streets had all learned his name. As he approached they all called out, "Sluggo! Here, darlin'—here sweetheart! You're such a handsome boy," and Sluggo dropped his leash from his mouth so he could lick hands and smirk.

It only took five minutes to get to the store and back but it could just as likely be twenty minutes or more depending on how many of Sluggo's friends were out on the pavement. These were some very tough women, even the youngest of them. Street whoring is a brutal life and it occurred to me that a short visit from Sluggo was as close to genuine love and affection, given and returned, as most of them ever got, and that between the johns and the cell-like rooms in the skid row hotels they came home to, it must be an unutterably lonely life. I suppose they could have had a goldfish but I don't know how much consolation coming home to a goldfish would be.

At least we had one handsome dog in the family. I wasn't making a good impression on anyone down there. One hot afternoon I volunteered to buy beer for the crew and Sluggo and I headed up the street to the Astoria Hotel. We came back with Sluggo as usual in the lead and me bringing up the rear with four six-packs, two in my hands and the other pair under my arms. It had been a long, sweltering day and I was covered in sweat, drywall dust, and general filth. I was wearing an old sleeveless black T-shirt, cut-off jeans and ratty sneakers and my hair was limp and wet and hanging down in my face. I had also come down a ladder that afternoon and twisted my ankle on a piece of scrap wood so I was lurching along on a gimpy leg, walking like a ninety-year-old sharecropper.

When I got to the corner Sluggo had already crossed to visit his girls and he was accepting tribute and compliments outside the 20-Hour Market while I waited for the light to change. I put the beer down and wiped my face on the hem of my shirt and pushed my hair back, just in time to see a family in a minivan pull up to the crosswalk, the mother pointing me out to two teenaged kids leaning over from the backseat. Maybe they brought them down to this part of town once in a while as a cautionary exercise, maybe they were just lost. Either way, Mom was not going to let this teachable moment pass.

I could read her lips unmistakably: "Look at that poor old man," she mouthed. The kids were wide-eyed, seeing themselves some years and a few Bad Choices down the road, brought low by liquor and Christ knows what, standing in torn and wretched shoes, lank dirty hair hanging off their brow, waiting for the light to change so they could hobble across. They stared at me from behind the air-conditioned windows, *tsk tsk tsk*, and I stared back. Then the light changed and they pulled away while Sluggo barked at me to hurry up from across the street.

When I say he was good, I do him a disservice. He was better than that, he was a paragon of intelligence and obedience. He even stopped pushing to get into the front seat of the car and sat happily in the cargo hold. It felt like I had grown another arm.

When we walked to the Chinese market he no longer barked madly and incessantly when I tied him to a parking meter, instead standing patiently until I came out.

He even stopped what we called The Revenge of Sluggo. If we went out without him, when we came back there would be a pile of dog-logs by the door. "He has issues," Lynda said. It was like saying Pol Pot was capricious.

He came to the studio with me and lay in the control room while we worked, dining on pieces of pizza and other takeaway food the musicians fed him on their breaks. He was an active partner in the business. Between the feeding and petting, meal and cigarette breaks took twice as long with him around, with the clock ticking all the while.

But he never lost that sparkle of pure hell in his eye and he still stood with his head slightly cocked and a devilish grin pasted on it. Experts will tell you different but I truly believe that dogs smile the same way we do, and for the same reasons. This was like the smile from a federal revenue agent, not a warning or a promise but a cold fact: "Here comes trouble."

Except that now it didn't. From that summer on he was the best dog you could ask for, as if he'd taken Mark Twain's advice to "always do right—this will gratify some and astonish the rest."

He did, however, retain a dog's sense of propriety. One day while I was doing yardwork in the front a "cognitively challenged" woman from one of the neighbourhood group homes came down the sidewalk and *Ohhhh*'d when she saw Sluggo. He knew a soft touch when he saw one and went out onto the sidewalk to be admired. She was wearing a pink kangaroo top and matching pink velour sweatpants, hiked up to the very limit, so that her lady parts were right out there in stark relief. "Can I pet your dog?" she asked, and I said: "Sure, he's friendly."

She put her hand out to rub his ear and Sluggo drove his snout into her crotch so enthusiastically half his head disappeared. She went up on her tiptoes and her eyebrows disappeared under her bangs. She squealed again and looked at me with her eyes wide: "Geez, he *is* friendly."

*Chapter Eleven*

# Another Death in the Family

*For that which befalleth the sons of men befalleth beasts; even one thing befalleth them: as the one dieth, so dieth the other; yea, they have all one breath; so that a man hath no preeminence above a beast: for all is vanity. All go unto one place; all are of the dust, and all turn to dust again.*

(ECCLESIASTES 3:19–20)

The summer after we moved to the downtown houses I turned forty-seven years old and Lynda and I decided to split up. After a dozen years together we were a couple only out of habit and the years were ticking by with increasing speed. Finally we looked at each other and said, "Why are we doing this?" Neither one of us had a good answer and so early in September two friends came over and we moved my things across the garden into the small back house. Lynda stayed in the main floor of the big house in front, with tenants in the basement.

Lynda kept the cats, Scruffy and Mouse, a foundling

we'd taken in. Sluggo came with me although he headed for Lynda's back stairs and his bowl of milk every morning when I let him out. Scruffy the white cat visited often and I ran a board from my kitchen window down to the side path so he could get in and out without having to depend on an unreliable human doorman.

It was a sad time and we were all hurting and a little off our game. One night while Sluggo and I were on the couch watching TV a mouse ran across the floor directly in front of Scruff, who barely raised his head to look. The mouse continued into the kitchen and we all watched for half an hour while he stole kibble from Sluggo's dish and ferried it behind the stove, one piece at a time. Every so often he would stop and look at us, whiskers twitching and eyes glittering, expecting surely someone would do something, but we just sat there, indifferent. Help yourself, Mr. Mouse. Come again. It's a hard world for everyone and who were we to begrudge a little grey mouse just trying to feed his family?

But life continues on and the days go by and the stars come up and the moon goes round. The tenants in the basement of the big house paid the bulk of the mortgage so Sluggo and I could live cheaply. The weather turned to endless damp greyness broken three or four days a week by heavy rain and it suited our mood.

I stayed in my writing room and came out to walk Sluggo or watch a basketball game on TV. I spoke to few people unless I had to and did most of my conversing with Sluggo. He was an attentive and sympathetic listener and never gave unwanted advice. He was content to commiserate and put his head across my lap while we lay on the couch and considered Big Questions. Invariably there were no answers and we climbed the stairs at night and crawled into bed, his head on one pillow and mine on the other.

It was a long, long winter and neither of us would have been surprised if it never ended but one day it did. The skies cleared, things came to life in the garden and the birds sang like madmen on the telephone wires. Things were looking up, it seemed, but the gods saw it all and laughed out loud.

One morning after feeding him his milk Lynda came across the yard and said there was a lump on one of Sluggo's legs. I called him over and he stood there happily while we both gave it a feel. It didn't seem to be bothering him but we took him up to the vet. They called a few days later to tell me it was a malignant tumour and we made an appointment that afternoon to discuss "treatment options."

There weren't any, really. There was no telling how far the cancer had spread and no guarantee that even if they took the leg it wasn't already racing though his body. An amputation is a very tough thing for even a healthy animal to recover from and we were just as likely to be putting him through it only to see him die anyway. The vet said he'd do it, if it was what we wanted, but he couldn't recommend it. The best thing we could do was to keep him happy, medicate the pain when it finally came, and enjoy what time we had left together. He gave me a prescription and we walked him from his office, Sluggo with his leash in his mouth, turning to make sure I was following him. I wondered how many walks we had left.

My wife had left me, my dog had cancer and I was out of work. I couldn't help but feel like I was living in a country and western song. But the worst of it all was being with Sluggo and wondering how long he had left, though he went without any symptoms other than the growing lump on his leg for weeks and weeks, as happy as ever.

Then he did start to limp slightly. I began his pain meds and the limp went away. The days followed with no real decline and I began to think the vet had been mistaken. We spent Christmas Day in our little house on skid row listening to the crazy people screaming on the sidewalk out front and the homeless ones chattering and lining up in the alley under my writing room window for turkey dinner at the mission up the street. We ate ours in front of the TV, switching back and forth between Alastair Sim in *A Christmas Carol* and the Christmas Day basketball games. All I wanted was a few more years of my dog. Like a lot of other people, I didn't get what I asked for.

Then it was early spring and there was no lying to myself. Sluggo was still happy and ready to start the day when we woke up but I had to help him up onto the bed at night. The tumour had lain fallow for some time but like the buds on the trees and the shoots in the garden beds it was coming back to life. It had stayed golf-ball-sized for months but now swelled to the size of a large peach. The vet adjusted his meds again, although he still wasn't show any signs of pain except for a slight limp. The vet said it was likely the cancer had eaten through the bone. My dog was on the downhill run and picking up speed.

About that time I started a new job. Things were getting tight; the medicine was expensive and the studio made no real money. In the fall I'd sold my library, collected over thirty years, and got a cheque for three thousand dollars. It was hard to say goodbye to them, collected over thousands of hours in used bookstores, poking endlessly through shelves and boxes for buried treasure and sometimes even finding it: Fitzgerald's Pat Hobby stories entombed for years at the bottom of a box of moldering encyclopedias, A.J. Liebling's *The Telephone Booth Indian* stranded on a high, never-visited shelf.

Sluggo and I lived on the proceeds for months and filled in the gaps with credit card advances. By March I was about ready to start selling guitars when a friend of a friend called and said he'd heard I was looking for work. Did I want some shifts as a "respite worker" in juvenile residential resources? I said yes, although I had no idea what he was talking about.

The next day I got a call asking if I could meet with one of the company's managers to talk about the job. We met at a coffee shop in the suburbs and he ran it down in short order. The government ministry responsible for childcare had cases where placing these kids with foster families wouldn't work because the "youth in care" were too "high behaviour" for a normal family to cope with. It was the first industry euphemism I came across and soon learned it meant "violent and crazy."

The youths had a litany of syndromes, disorders, and troubles—fetal alcohol syndrome, ADHD, paranoid schizophrenia, Tourette's syndrome, multiple drug addictions, Asperger's syndrome, oppositional defiance disorder, sexual abuse, physical abuse, and any combination of these and others. Their case files were a compendium of medical and psychological acronyms and medication attempts. The only other options were jail, where they would surely land if left where they were, or a locked psychiatric ward.

Instead the ministry paid tens of thousands of dollars a month for these children to be housed in an artificial home environment. As a result, the company was always looking for new caregivers. There was a high turnover among the staff, enough so that after a twenty-minute conversation the man asked me if I'd brought my toothbrush. He needed me to start right now—one of his caregivers had quit that day after being chased down the street by a psychotic thirteen-year-old with a carving knife, and the rest of the staff badly needed time off. The shifts were twenty-four hours and paid $150.

I ended up working nine days straight and Lynda

brought Sluggo out to join me. There were two caregivers on duty with this boy at all times, by court
order—he had an alphabet soup of ills and a two-page
meds sheet detailing the dozen pills he was on to hold
them at bay. He was the patient as barn door and they
were throwing drugs at him with both hands to see
what stuck.

None of them seemed to give him or anyone else
much relief; the police had to be called two or three
times a day when he assaulted a staff member or ran
out into the street and attacked passersby. Many times
as I was doling out his pills it was all I could do to keep
from taking a handful myself. The company found
that once caregivers left the place for a day off and
re-experienced sanity in the real world, they couldn't
bring themselves to come back. New bodies replaced
them and within a couple of weeks I was the senior
caregiver.

In the third month the boy finally went after me
with the leg from the dining room table and I wrestled him down and pinned him while someone called
the police. When the officer tried to talk to him, he
went after the cop, too, and wound up face down
and handcuffed before I had enough time to raise my
eyebrows.

I expected to be let go but the contract for his care
was still in effect and—unlikely as it was he would
be released any time soon—the ministry needed to
know there was place for him to go if he got out. For
their part the company was happy to leave the house

open and keep cashing the cheques. For the next six weeks Sluggo and I lived in a five bedroom house by ourselves.

I visited my client when I was allowed to, if he wasn't in isolation for attacking anyone that day, and took him magazines though he begged for cigarettes. During in-between times Sluggo and I went to the park up the street and he chased squirrels and birds, his bad leg flopping behind him as he ran. He came with me the seven or eight blocks to the grocery store and back again, with rest stops along the way. I wrote in the staff room with Sluggo on the bed behind me and we watched TV on the couch, his head on my lap. We were the last ones standing and worked straight through until the boy was formally committed. By the time the government machine processed this and cancelled the contract for his care I had paid off my bills.

It had been strange and disorienting, like the way veterans describe combat, long periods of boredom broken by sudden episodes of sheer terror. Even so, I dreaded closing the place up and going home. I knew too well what was coming.

From the day he was diagnosed I devoted twenty minutes or so every morning to petting and scratching and talking to Sluggo. I talked to him about what we were going to do that day and where we were going. He soaked it up like the love sponge he'd always been, sighing in contentment and rolling over for a long belly massage. When we were done I patted him twice on the rump, the long-time signal to leap up, tail stump wagging like a broken propeller, and jump off the bed. As he got worse he began to step down off it using just his front feet and then hopping down the rest of the way with his good leg. This morning our cuddle time lasted almost an hour, me looking constantly at the clock that was moving too fast. We had an appointment with the vet and I was scratching his ears and rubbing his stomach for the last time, watching his good leg quiver and jerk with happiness.

Once again I lay down on the floor and held my dog while the vet prepared a needle full of murder. I rubbed his ears and talked quietly to him. He'd had the sedation and was breathing easy in my arms, his leg shaved and waiting. I could see my ugly puppy still there, far too young to die, but aren't we all?

I remembered the first time we took him for a walk, so tiny and clumsy he could barely get up and down the curb of the sidewalk. When I looked into his eyes they were still full of the love and intelligence and pure devilry that made him who he was. I knew I would never again see him look back at me over his shoulder, leash hanging from his mouth, impatiently waiting for me to catch up.

I buried my head in his shoulder and tried not to start crying until he'd stopped breathing. Then I tucked his tongue back into his mouth where it had fallen loose as he relaxed into eternity and left me forever. I miss him every day of my life.

Why, I sometimes wonder. Why Sluggo even more than Rip or Mugsy? Part of it has to be that after the divorce he was my only company for months. Sluggo and I talked about everything. We had long conversations about what to have for dinner, what we saw on our daily walks to the Chinese vegetable market to buy the one-dollar bags of "slightly irregular" vegetables I used to make soups, stews, and pasta sauce. I told him about problems with what I was writing and he commiserated. When I shouted at an exceptional play during the basketball game on TV, he celebrated, too. When I decried a bad call, he sulked along with me. He answered me with head cocked, one ear up. His eyes squinted if he wasn't buying it and opened wide when I had good news.

One of my friends came by a few months after the divorce and said he was worried about me spending all this time alone. "Alone?" I said. "I've got Sluggo." We knew each other better than anyone else ever could.

Maybe that's the answer; every time I lost a dog I had another dog to give my love to, or at least a person with me to share the grief. This time it was just the two of us, and then it was just me.

*Chapter Twelve*

# City Dog / Country Dog

The world seemed very small without Sluggo in it and the tiny house was enormous. I cried in the morning when I got up and cried again when I climbed the narrow stairs to bed, alone. It rained for days on end and I only left the house to buy food. Vancouver is in a coastal rainforest and spring is the rainy season. Well, one of them—we have several. The others are winter and fall and part of the summer.

My best friend was gone but there was no shortage of messed-up kids. I was offered another job from the same agency, this time with two boys. One was a fourteen-year-old burglar and sex criminal who had to be kept away from younger girls. The other was a giant autistic boy of seventeen.

A house needed to be found, rented and furnished, the kids registered for school, if one could be found that would take them, and a staff hired. When I finally got a few days off I came home to a note on my door from the tenant in the basement of Lynda's house. He knew someone with a year-old Rottweiler he couldn't keep. Call this number if interested and ask for Ronald.

That afternoon a huge, silver-haired biker covered in tattoos knocked on my door and introduced me to Bobo, a lanky and slightly goofy young dog. Ronald and I sat down to talk and Bobo jumped up on the couch beside me and lay down with his head on my leg. He'd been rescued from an abusive home and Ronald was fostering him but he couldn't keep him permanently. He lived on the ground floor of a warehouse where he could ride his bike straight off the street and through the door. It was a huge open space but he already had two Rottis, and while he looked quite capable of either starting or ending a small war by himself, a pack of dogs in his house was more than he could handle.

"Two is doable," he said. He sat down on the arm of a chair and uncapped a beer, "But get the third one in there and they just chase each other around the place all day at full speed. I've seen them run up the damn walls. Then they take off again in the other direction. If something's in the way they just run right over it." He took a swallow. "I hate to give the little guy up but it's just . . . too much to deal with. The place is a disaster every time I come home."

My neighbour had vouched for me and Ronald trusted that assessment enough to leave the dog with me if I wanted. I did. At the gate, he turned to ruffle Bobo's ears and I could see tears running down the big man's face. "Come back and visit him whenever you want," I said.

"I don't think I'd be able to do that," he said, turning away and walking quickly down the sidewalk away from us.

In the ten years since then Bobo and I have been apart less than two weeks, total.

The contract manager at the home had no problem with me bringing a dog to work so Bobo came with me and even seemed to be good for the boys. Four days a week he came with me to the new house and we were never more than a few feet apart, twenty-four hours a day. When I cooked, he was in the kitchen. When I was in the office, he was on the bed watching me. When I did the shopping he waited in the car or patiently outside.

As testament to Bobo's goodwill toward all beings, he never once snapped or became seriously annoyed with any of the boys, though there were times I was ready to bury either or both of them in a shallow grave in the backyard.

The seventeen-year-old boy—along with his other problems—had sexual impulse control issues; as in, he had none. Already somewhat menacing with his size and the disturbing grin that was his default facial expression, Li shaved his head and wore round wire-rim glasses and affected a tiny, sparse moustache, the combination of which gave him a startling resemblance to Sinister Oriental character actors of the 1940s. With his pants pulled up to his ribcage and his belt pulled several notches too tight, carrying a child's book bag, he looked like he had killed and eaten the child and was

140

now looking for a place to dispose of the bag.

He was the only "youth," as we were instructed to refer to them, who Bobo ever lost patience with. When he got too close Bobo would move away and growl softly, almost under his breath, which seemed very unlike him until the other boy said, "When you guys are out of the house, he touches Bobo"—he paused and adopted a serious, adult manner— "inappropriately..."

It had never occurred to me that his sex mania extended to interspecies romance. When there was a problem later with Li qualifying for disability payments, I suggested to his social worker that she tell them he tried to sexually assault a Rottweiler. That sounded like unassailable proof of diminished capacity to me.

Four nights a week Bobo and I shared the double bed in the staff quarters and Friday morning we packed the duffel bag and came home for three days, where things continued much the same. When I made bacon and eggs in the morning I poured the liquid grease on his kibble and whatever I cooked for dinner, he got the leftovers. He peed in the garden, and so did I on occasion. Things went on this way for a couple of years. I avoided human relationships; when I wasn't working I read and wrote and kept to myself. This went on for about two years. Then Penny came along and everything changed.

We met online and after a month or two of serious emailing, she came into town for dinner and ended up staying the night. Bobo seemed fine with this at first, though he did stake out a rather large chunk of the bed and refuse to move when asked — this was after I was asleep.

Between my weird little tumbledown house on skid row and the massive dog who had his own seat on the couch for watching TV, ate at the table and slept in the bed, I can't imagine why she came back, but she did and Bobo began to make an issue of who ranked where in the social order. When she came out the back door of the big house where she still lived and across the garden to my house Bobo would stand at the top of the porch and wag his tail while growling at her. It was a schizophrenic welcoming, and it left her as confused as Bobo.

Once I escorted her in he was all smiles and they got along famously but come bedtime there was a struggle over real estate that was never fully resolved. We finally settled on a system where I slept in the middle of the bed, between them. Both of them are highly affectionate and tend to sprawl over me so if I had to get up in the night there was only a long, narrow burrow between them when I came back, requiring me to essentially screw myself back into the bedcovers.

I thought a king-size bed would give us all a little more room but it only meant they both glommed onto me like a piece of flotsam after a shipwreck and the three of us made a pile of bodies on one side of the bed while the other remained vacant and maddeningly out of reach. If I tried to sneak out to the wide open spaces they both crawled and flopped after me like blind kittens towards the mother cat. There is no escape, and I've reconciled myself to it.

The other thing we've had to learn to live with is Bobo's insistence on always being in the room with us, whether we're sleeping or using the bed for other things. When I was young, I loved to jump on the bed as though it were a trampoline and, of course, my mother forbade it. One night I woke up and heard muffled happy noises and the unmistakeable sounds of a bed being jumped on. I crept quietly down the hall, then threw the bedroom door open and shouted, "I caught you!" They looked very guilty and I still think it was unfair that although they were the ones jumping on the bed, *I* was punished.

Bobo has the same suspicion if we close the bedroom door. He knows we're doing something fun in there, probably eating sandwiches, and demands to be let in. No matter how many times we let him in and he finds nothing, he remains convinced we have a picnic hamper in there. I'm now closely watched during what were, previously, intimate acts. If things ever get so bad I have to go into porn, at least I have some experience with performing to an audience.

Penny lived in farm country, about a hundred miles outside the city. Between her schedule and mine we could only see each other once a week. When my company offered me a new position doing the same work

fifteen minutes from Penny's doorstep, I took it. Bobo
and were moving to Chilliwack, a small town surrounded by mountains at the eastern end of the Fraser
Valley.

I had to have a "youth resource" open in Chilliwack
for the first of the month, find tenants for my place
in Vancouver, unload about half my possessions, pack
what was left and organize the move while still working ninety-six hours a week at the home I was currently
employed at. It was a lightning move, as if we were
dodging the landlord. God knows I'd done enough of
those but never one from a house I actually owned.

We made it by the skin of our teeth and left Vancouver in a snowstorm late on January 31st with my old
'69 Mercedes jammed to the roof with Bobo, Penny
and I, and the last boxes and oddments that are always
left over for the final load of any move — the lid to the
teapot, a cribbage board, assorted plants and pictures.
We pulled away from the curb with the trunk half-
open and tied down with a bungee cord. We looked
like Okies fleeing the dustbowl for California, except
that we had a Rottweiler hanging out the back window
biting at snowflakes.

That night we slept at a motel and the next morning
I met the movers at the house Penny had found for
us. It had two bedrooms upstairs and a fully contained
suite downstairs, which I could flee to when I was off-
shift. And this is where the war between Penny and
Bobo really began.

When I say "war" I'm overstating it. Some feelings

have been badly bruised but there have been no casualities. There have been some harsh words and threats from both sides but no intentional violence—although Bobo did break her big toe in the regrettable Front Door Incident. Deadly gas has been deployed but does that really count if the perpetrator has no idea he's doing it and continues to snore on the carpet? No, this exceedingly civil war hinges on Penny's assertion that Bobo is a dog, and his—and my—refutation of the premise. I contend that he's a family member who happens to share the physical characteristics of a dog while Bobo rejects the notion *in toto*, as the lawyers say.

The first shots were fired over whether Bobo should eat at the table or not. Before Penny, I'd been in the habit of buying a bit more than I needed, an extra pork chop or a larger steak, and giving Bobo his share—fortunately we both liked our steak medium rare. The first time Penny saw me do this she nearly swallowed her tongue in an apoplectic fit. Not that he actually ever ate "at the table"—he didn't sit in a chair or have a place setting. He sat on the floor across from my chair and ate the bits I gave him. At our old house he sat on the other side of the table and I threw the food to him, a game we both enjoyed but which Penny objected to strongly. Her then eleven-year-old son Fergus saw this and argued that we should all eat this way, throwing the food to each other across the table. He and Bobo found limited support for the plan. I could have gone either way, but this practice is now also ended, and I feel guilty every time I cook meat and see Bobo watching me, the sharp hurt of betrayal in his eyes.

A compromise was reached where Bobo now lays on the floor beside my chair. Someone reaching for their glass or another potato may still find their hand blocked or their elbow bumped by a large black furry head, resting on its chin at the edge of the table, snout laid across the wood like some suckling pig, lacking only an apple in his jaws. How he insinuates himself there with no one noticing is a mystery. None of us have seen him in the process. He is either on the floor or his face is there on the table, patiently waiting for something to roll off a plate.

The dinner table edict was only the opening salvo. Once Penny and I had a house of our own she began to rewrite the rulebook and the most contentious change was No Dogs On the Bed. Bobo had slept on the bed with me every night since we'd met and to be suddenly led over to a cushion on the floor and told to lie down on it was heartbreaking. He wasn't very happy about it either and for months I would wake up and see his great head resting on the covers and staring at me with a pitiful look in his eyes.

*How can you do me like this?* he's saying, and I have no answer. Instead, torn between loyalties, I have become an accomplice, a contemptible quisling.

Penny leaves for work at 6:30 and at 6:31 Bobo is on the bed. At first he waited until he heard her car starting but after a few weeks he said *the hell with it* and just hopped up as soon as she kissed me and shut the door on her way out. That was fine until we replaced the old wall-to-wall carpet with shiny new laminate flooring. Bobo can't get any real traction on it and he trots back and forth from her side of the bed to mine, looking for an easier way up.

The laminate has caused all kinds of problems for him and he much preferred the sure footing the horrible, stained wall-to-wall gave him. Now, when he hears someone at the door, he can never remember that while he can get his legs whirling like a high-speed turbine and eventually gather a head of steam, he has no more ability to stop or corner than a 4x4 on an icy road.

When he does try to stop and goes into an uncontrollable skid, flying full-tilt down the hallway with a concerned look in his eye, he reminds me of a '65 Mustang I had. In winter, the combination of icy roads and the overpowered 289 engine meant that if you forgot yourself and gunned the engine, seeing the rear end come around and pass you as you went into a series of doughnuts was a common event. Likewise, Bobo usually sees the nub of his tail overtaking him shortly before his wild ride ends abruptly at a wall with a house-rattling thump. It leads to some worried looks when we finally get him out of the way and open the door for the visitor, and unlike my old car, it can't be solved by throwing a bunch of cinderblocks in his trunk.

In the morning, the clicking of his nails on the slick boards as he paces around the bed looking for a way up is sufficiently annoying that I have no choice but to get up, open the bedroom door so he can get a run at it from the hallway, and then get back in for another hour's sleep.

This works fine Monday to Friday but come Saturday Penny still wakes early and considers eight o'clock shamefully late. After making her coffee she comes back to the bedroom and she and Bobo square off. I huddle in a lump, under the covers, and try to avoid becoming collateral damage.

"Bobo, get down," she says in a quiet, firm voice.

"Grrrrrrr," Bobo says, equally quiet, equally firm.

"Get down."

"Grrrrrrrrrrrrrrrrrrrr." A slight change in pitch, dropping at the end. This is the equivalent of *Can't you take a hint?*

"Bobo bear, get down." This is like a mother using the full name of a child to indicate her displeasure . . .

"GRRRRRRrrrrrrrrrrrrr." *Now you're starting to get on my nerves.*

This continues until eventually Bobo capitulates, slinking off the bed an inch at a time and often hanging there, feet on the floor but with his rear end still up on the bed, growling with increasing vigour while Penny hovers over him. Back in Vancouver when he stood at the top of my steps and growled at her, he had some leverage because she didn't really know him yet and believed he might be capable of biting her. But those days are long gone. The growling is just an attempt to save face—he knows he's getting off the bed, she knows it, and I know I'm going to have to answer for my part in how he got up there in the first place.

My justification is that he's also been banned from the new leather couch, for reasons I can't argue. So it's all been taken away—the steak, the table, the bed, the couch—what's next, he has to run behind the car when we go out instead of riding in the back seat?

She's turned him into a dog, and even worse, he's her dog. He goes from window to window looking for her car as 6:00 p.m. approaches and he runs down to the garage to meet her. If she's late he lies on the concrete and pines like Greyfriars Bobby on the grave of his master.

Not that he loves me any less; dogs are capable of loving an indeterminate number of people completely, without reservation or ranking. Some people claim to be able to do the same thing but it generally ends in tears, and lawyers. Like licking your privates on the living room floor, polyamory is best left to those expressly built for it.


Along with Penny I also got, at no extra charge, two teenage kids and a spare dog. I'm used to having two dogs and I've developed skills specific to the situation. I can pet ambidextrously, using one hand for each dog, or if Seamus lays down I can rub his belly with my foot while scratching Bobo; after ten minutes of this I feel qualified to plays drums in a jazz band.

Seamus is my stepdog, who we board for up to a week at a time when Penny's ex-husband is travelling. He's a sweet mutt and a fine example of the genus

Medium-Sized Brown Dog, a Labrador and who-the-hell-knows cross, possibly wolverine. Brown Dogs are a distinct breed and so alike they're practically interchangeable, much like Black Cats. (Once I saw my Black Cat, Mousie, calmly sitting on a porch across the street when I lived in downtown Vancouver. It was a busy, dangerous road and I ran across it dodging cars to retrieve her. She seemed more than a little anxious when I scooped her up and ran back to safety, giving her a stern talking-to all the way. By the time I got up our steps she was clawing at me frantically and it was then that I saw Mousie sitting on the top step looking at me with her usual expression of mild contempt and disinterest. The cat in my arms bit me hard and leaped away, running back through the traffic to her own home, and from that day on hid under the bushes in her yard every time I walked past.)

One trait Brown Dogs share is the Low Table-Clearing Tail. This is coupled with Immediate Wagging Syndrome and it's a dangerous combination. It takes almost nothing to make Seamus wag his tail—look at him and he starts his motor; say his name and he goes into high gear. This leads to unfortunate situations. Seamus will pass through the area between the couch and coffee table, tail at a moderate rotation, and someone on the couch, seeing drinks and popcorn about to go flying, will say, "Seamus, go!" or "Seamus, move!" It doesn't matter what you say so long as his name is in there—"Seamus" and "The sum of the square roots of any two sides of an isosceles triangle is equal to the square root of the remaining side"—and the tail is instantly activated, everything on the table swept away at slap-shot velocity. Then come the angry words—"Bad dog, Seamus" thoroughly confuses him—and Seamus is left to wonder how things went wrong so fast.

It is impossible for him, or us, to learn anything from this tragic example of action and reaction. In the end Seamus eats whatever he flung onto the carpet and wags some more in happiness. There may be an element of positive reinforcement here; Rip used to clear tables with his tail and eat and drink the spillage, but once he figured out that anything that hit the floor was his he streamlined the process by simply pushing drinks and bowls onto the floor with his nose. He trained us—we instinctively grabbed for and held onto things with one hand whenever he came near. I dread the day Seamus figures this out for himself.

Seamus was raised in the small village of Yarrow, where even today horses are as common on the street as cars and road signs instruct you to "Respect Farm Vehicles." In Yarrow, nature's cruel drama is played out constantly. The days are filled with hawks, eagles, falcons, and great herons wheeling through the sky and deer, skunks, and the occasional bear and cougar in the backyard, and the night is filled with shrieks and howls.

Murder is a way of life out here and Seamus is a killer, pure and simple. There is no malice or cruelty in him. He simply likes the taste of blood and he knows where to find it—inside things. He was built to kill, every inch specifically designed for the job and no doubt about it. He goes about his work with a smile on his face and a happy song in his heart; if he could whistle while he worked, he would.

One time he climbed fifteen feet into an apple tree to get at a cat and the cat about had a nervous breakdown. It seemed terribly unfair to him that his entire life he had been raised to take the high ground and sneer at the dog below, and now this hound of hell was three branches below him and licking his chops.

The cat finally got himself out to the thinnest branches at the top of the tree and clung there, puffed up to twice normal size, every hair on his body standing straight up, swaying like a child's balloon on a string. They might be there still but we coaxed Seamus down eventually and he had no more trouble getting out of the tree than he did getting up it. The cat stayed there for hours before he judged it safe to come down and when he did he hit the ground running. *Sweet Jesus, you'll never believe what happened to me today . . .*

It reminded me of the time I saw two crows lure a cat into a tree and then play with him, letting him get closer and closer before hopping up a few more branches, the cat slithering along the limbs like a snake, ears and body flat as rain on a sidewalk. When he got close again the birds cawed at each other and moved up some more until the cat was at the very top of the tree, swinging back and forth precariously on a slender twig, at which point the birds flew to the telephone pole and laughed long and loud while the cat tried to figure out how to turn around. Don't ever mess with a crow.

Bobo was raised much differently, of course. Seamus can hear a rustle in the bushes and have the critter in his jaws before the poor thing realizes it's being eaten. Bobo will hear it too, but he stands there waiting for it to come out and play. As far as he's concerned food comes from a cupboard and he can hear the opener or the rustle of a bag from miles away. Seamus is by nature and nurture more equipped to deal with life in the wild but Bobo is equally well-equipped to thrive in his world—at least, he hasn't missed any meals. Seamus will happily eat whatever you give him though he would prefer it with the heart still beating and steam rising from the hot blood if possible.

The difference in them is best illustrated by the day we took them both to the river. It was fall and we wanted to see the salmon spawning. By the time they make it upriver they tend to be in sad shape and nearly dead, rotting flesh falling from their bones. Happily, this is just the way Seamus likes his salmon.

He ran at full gallop into the water, biting and tearing chunks of fish. It was a seafood buffet and playground all in one. He tore great chunks of flesh and then threw them in the air over his head. Bobo had no idea what was going on and stood on the shore and barked. Seamus stared at him in bafflement and finally bit into a large salmon and carried it to Bobo, dropping it at his feet. He stood there wagging his tail and grinning—*Go on, have some. It's good.*

Bobo sniffed it and looked back at him. The fish

flopped in a final convulsion and Bobo leaped back in fright. Seamus shook his head and went back to the water. Bobo stuck with me. He eventually worked himself up to go down to the shallows but whenever a fish twitched and jumped he ran back to us. While Seamus chased the more mobile salmon through the runnels at the edge of the riverbank Bobo barked madly, cheering him on, but from a safe distance.

Seamus has his blind spots, too. He cannot be cured of escaping and if anyone is foolish enough to open the door without blocking it there will be a terrific whooshing of air akin to someone opening the airlock on a spaceship. Seamus can reach escape velocity from anywhere in the house, standing, sitting, or lying down, and be through the door and gone from sight immediately. You can follow for him for hours and he will stay just this much ahead of you in a cruel game that keeps you going but never gets you close enough to grab him.

This can go on for hours unless you go back to the driveway, open the car door and slam it shut. When he hears that he'll race back from wherever he is so as not to miss out on a car ride. Simply let him get in and sit for a few seconds, then open the door again and he will follow you happily back into the house. As far as he's concerned he went for a ride.

All this talk of steak and salmon brings us to the continuing puzzle of what dogs will and won't eat, and the corollary question, how can dogs tell the difference between brands of pet food and emphatically approve or shun what appear to be identical products, yet at the same time be completely undiscerning about most other things they swallow?

I have seen my own dogs chew on a whitened, fossilized turd while out on a walk then come home and turn their noses up at the food I put in the bowl, looking up at me with a deeply sorrowful and disappointed expression. When I had both dogs and cats there was a running battle trying to keep the former out of the latter's litter box, where they believed little Oh Henry! bars had been hidden under the sand, like some scatological Easter hunt.

Cat turds aren't even close to the strangest things dogs will eat. A news service asked readers to send in examples of things their dogs had eaten and among the responses were:

Paul Miele, a man from Pittsburgh, had a Shepherd/Rottweiler mix who ate three-foot sheets of carpet underlay and the tack-strip to go with it, effectively doing a wall-to-wall renovation of his innards, and on another occasion a box of macaroni dinner, including the grocery bag, the cardboard box, and foil package of cheese sauce.

One dog ate the branches of an artificial Christmas tree, another ignored the branches but ate the ornaments, with no result except for sparkly dog deposits on the lawn. Another swallowed a string of Christmas lights which were retrieved, as was the fringe holding a throw rug together.

"I pulled it out of his butt like a magician pulls scarves from his sleeve," said the owner, from South Portland, Maine, who did not wish to be identified.

Lighters, bras, batteries, cell phones, golf balls, electrical cords, a carton of cigarettes, a full bottle of Motrin, another of Prozac, rolls of tinfoil, a sleeping bag, action figures, Tupperware bowls, soda bottles and cans, a tin of cat food—unopened—Brillo pads, swim suits, toilet rolls, a bottle of green food dye with the expected result, a parakeet which went down whole and came out that way, too. The owner says the bird was never really himself afterwards. Who would be?

Mugsy once ate an entire chicken my roommate Jason had cooked and left to cool on the counter, planning to make a week's worth of sandwiches from it. He turned to do something else and when he looked back Mugs already had it in his mouth, and he ended up chasing him around the yard for a good ten minutes before Mugs finally let it go, at which point it wasn't really good for much.

But Mugs concentrated on actual foodstuffs. When he did pick up shoes or books it was only so he could carry them around the house in his mouth. He never chewed them though they needed to be wrung out when he was done with them. Sluggo, though—he ate anything he could get into his mouth, and if it was too big to fit he tore pieces off and ate it in sections. Once, when we had an appliance repairman working in behind the fridge, he laid his tools out on the floor where he could reach back and grab them as he needed them. Sluggo picked them up in his mouth, one by one, and took them out in the yard to eat. He got the plastic ends of the screwdrivers off and crunched them up but the solid steel wrenches were harder going and I caught him just as he was burying the lot of them where I imagine he hoped they would soften up.

He did the same thing with smoked, dried pig's-ear treats and we were perpetually disinterring buried ears while gardening. The pig's ears were creepy enough to start with but because the ground was moist, they were rehydrated when you dug them up and there was an uncomfortable serial-killer feeling to the whole business.

Rip simply had an open-mouth policy. Anything on the ground was fair game: the quick and the dead, the inert, plastic, animal, vegetable, mineral (he liked to eat rocks, but only certain ones) it was all grist for his inner mill. He ate bugs happily, snapping at flies, launching himself around the house in summer like a 120-pound trout leaping out of the stream after a mosquito. The official first day of summer was marked by Rip's yelp from the backyard, which meant he had caught his first bee of the year.

When Rip was about four months old a friend was staying with us and woke up with the feeling something was wrong with his shoes and there was Rip, beside his bed, halfway through a hiking boot. My friend reached down and pulled the boot away from him, on principle alone as it was no longer of any real use to him, and Rip promptly bit him and took it back. Not a bad bite, just enough to let him know what was what, the way I might chastise a waiter who tried to remove my plate partway through the main course.

Eventually we taught Rip he was only allowed to chew things we gave to him, and from that point he never ate another shoe, coat, book, what have you. Before that, the house looked vacant from about twenty-four inches up the walls down to the floor boards, with everything else secured above that height, as if we lived in a campsite and had to hoist our possessions up out of the reach of midget bears.

Rip's joy of eating caused him considerable pain on occasion, the worst being the time my cousins up the coast gave my parents two great sacks of fresh prawns. We invited friends over for a feast and set garbage cans around the kitchen for the shells and heads. When the cans were full we took them outside, the remains to be dug into the garden later.

A few hours into the party I heard a terrible howling from the yard and ran out onto the porch, from which I could see Rip, squatted in the familiar pose and straining with a look of great concern in his eyes. He had, of course, gotten into the garbage and eaten who knows how many prawn shells, low on meat but still dripping butter and garlic. It was a rich dinner but now the bill was due. I could see his legs trembling with effort and he howled pitiably. I've heard people describe passing a kidney stone as the worst pain imaginable. Passing a few pounds of prawn skeletons and heads, all sharp angles and vicious pokey bits, must be right up there.

Rip gave a horrified yip as something finally came free and, in one of the most unforgettable sights of my life, I saw a prawn head emerge from his rear end, black eyes and waggling antennae first, as if it were chewing its way out from the inside. It was like something from the *Alien* films and a highly disturbing thing to see. Rip howled again and the thing popped out and lay on the lawn. Rip turned and sniffed at it nervously. He would have eaten it again but I pulled him away in time.

Bobo is the exception to the rule, a positively fastidious eater. He has never eaten an item of clothing, chewed the leg of a table, torn up a magazine, or shown any inclination at all to do so. The problem with him is figuring out what he does want to eat, and how he likes it. He often spurns bacon because he's simply not in the mood for it. He loves a nice mild curry but may or may not clean up a plate with gravy on it. He will beg for something, turning those brown soulful eyes on you until you tear off a bit of your apple, and then he will taste it and make up his mind. If it doesn't make the cut he will simply let it fall out of his mouth rather than do something so vulgar as to spit it out.

If I buy a brand of kibble he doesn't care for he can actually sort the chunks in his mouth so that the bits he doesn't like end up all over the floor, like some industrial sorting machine rejecting substandard Tootsie Rolls. Leftover salad on a dinner plate is a fair bet, and the odds are better if it has Thousand Island dressing on it, or perhaps ranch, but not fruity vinaigrettes, although a classic dressing of oil, vinegar and grated, sharp cheese is generally acceptable.

It's an unpredictable business and often contrary. Like Whitman, Bobo is unconcerned by it: *Do I contradict myself? Very well, then I contradict myself. I am large, I contain multitudes.*

Which brings us, unavoidably, to dog farts. Rip blamed his farts on me. He was a master of the silent, deadly expulsion and when it did make a sound, it was a loose, meaty rumble, like a trombone player working on his embouchure. They were thick and overwhelming, so pungent you could almost see them as a heavy, rank mist that made the eyes water so badly you might go dice an onion, very fine, just for relief. They were oddly reminiscent of burning plastic and spoiled Chinese food, the smell that hits you when you open an aluminum dish from the back of the fridge and try to remember the last time you ordered takeout. When Rip let one go he would prop his head up and look around, then nonchalantly swivel his head and take a sniff buttwards, then get up, look at me for a second as if to say, *Hey, don't look at me*, and leave the room.

People always ask why a dog loves to stick his head out the car window but hates when you blow in his face; I would rather know why he looks embarrassed while squatting to relieve himself but is absolutely nonchalant about letting one go in the living room while your in-laws are eating cheese and crackers.

Dog farts are as unique as fingerprints and should be used as a means of positive identification. The next time you find a lost dog without a name tag and post a "Found" notice, try this when someone answers your ad:

"Hello, you found a black lab near Foster Street? I think he's mine."

"Yes, we did. Can you describe what his farts smell like?"

"What?"

"Describe his farts—what do they smell like?"

(*Short pause.*) "Well . . . sort of like fermented cabbage with a whiff of mustard gas, damp earth in a crawl-space, old tires in the sun and a hint of cinnamon."

"Come and get him . . . "

Mugsy snored and farted while asleep, alternately, so that it was like sleeping in a room with some strange, steam-driven engine burning an evil fuel. First the rhythmic snores, in and out. They began as random snorts and lip-rippling expulsions as he nodded off, then settled into a regular, moderate-paced tempo that was oddly comforting, like the chatter of railcars rushing past. Then, when we were lulled into that warm, safe place just this side of deep sleep, his pneumonic lullaby was punctuated by great *blats* from the other end, horn blasts that the angel Gabriel would be proud of.

He had a repertoire of them, from alto to basso, diminuendo to colossale: deep, foghorn rumblings; sharp explosions like someone popping a paper bag filled with bad air; wet toots like a flute filled with mud; strings of Chinese firecrackers; and the dreaded *Pooooooooooooot*, as if someone had disregarded the warning signs and unsealed a hatch never meant to be opened.

The Poot was exactly that, a soft *poooot* and then the sound of air—*Pppphhhhhhhhhhhhhhhhhhhh*—and then the waiting, when nothing happened, just long enough for you to relax. Then, when it did come, it came on suddenly and whatever chemicals conspired in his guts to make this substance were much heavier than air and so it lay like a low, vile fog, just high enough to reach the bed. We hid under the covers, arms fumbling blindly for the window over the headboard. You had to breathe through your mouth but even then it was a terrible thing, so bad you'd brush your teeth with dirt just to get the taste out.

There was no particular food item that brought it on. Mugs ate table scraps his whole life, and kibble, and wet, canned dog food. There were several brands we tried once and immediately moved to the do-not-buy list but nothing we ever fed him could account for what came out.

I swear it changed the paint colour of the walls. They started out cloud white but by the time he died they were a sort of caramel. In my youth, people were quick to suggest lighting a match when someone let one go. This would serve little purpose in Mugsy's case—you'd need to set fire to the drapes, at the very least.

(Sluggo, oddly, never farted that I can recall. He

crapped on the floor when he was angry, if he'd been left behind for a car trip or mistreated in some other fashion.)

And Bobo? He's as bad as Rip and gaining on Mugsy as he grows older. There's no use describing them. Like getting a spinal tap or giving birth it can only be experienced. The only comment that ever came close to capturing the foulness of what comes out of him was by my daughter Nadia. Bobo was asleep at her feet while we watched a movie. There was a tell-tale *Phhrrrrrrrt* and soon we were engulfed. Pulling her sweater up over her face, Nadia cried, "Oh Bobo—why?" But like so many things in life, there was no answer.

At least Nadia could run away. Penny suffers from terminally cold feet and often when she's sitting on the couch Bobo lies across her feet, which is nice and warm, yes, but at what price? It leaves her chained to her place like a galley slave in a sinking ship when the dog inevitably lets one go. All she can do for protection is pull her sweater or housecoat up over her face, try to hold out and practice the yogic principle of "breathing through your eyes."

*Chapter Thirteen*

# Bobo's World

Dogs have been at war with vacuum cleaners since their first meeting, with no quarter asked and none given. It's easy for us to laugh but a stiff-legged dog squaring off against a roaring metal monster is an act of monumental bravery. He doesn't know he's only defending us from being able to walk around in bare feet or rescue errant toast slices from the floor and it's wrong to belittle his bravery. All he knows is that he is the last line of defence, standing between this howling threat and all he holds dear, and he's ready to die in his tracks to defend us.

Bobo, though, unlike every other dog I've known, never much cared about the vacuum. He gave it a cold glare when it came around the corner and when he moved to avoid it he often stopped and gave it a long look, as if to say *I'm watching you . . . govern yourself accordingly*.

Truth be told, Bobo is about as non-confrontational as they come. On a sliding scale of aggression, he would be down there with caterpillars and seahorses, even below small birds and turtles, both of whom are far more likely to bite you.

No, like most of us Bobo's first impulse is towards coexistence. If that fails he prefers to—it would be mean-spirited to describe it as "running away"—more, "withdraw with all due expedience and consider the options." As the options are generally eating or sleeping on the couch, this is not a lengthy process and Bobo has found that most often by the time he's had something to eat and a nice nap, the problem has resolved itself. He is one of the few Rottweilers to have so thoroughly adopted the notion of laissez faire. But that all changed when we bought Dave.

Dave is a robot vacuum, about the circumference and depth of a small stack of medium frozen pizzas. He does not roar and carry on like a standard vacuum but he does beep intermittently and, on occasion, speaks in a somewhat zombified female voice, as in "Clean my brushes." Or, when he climbs the chrome legs of the lounge chair and can't get back down, "Unspecified error!"

Despite its feminine voice the vacuum is named Dave in honour of my friend Dave Watson, a great believer in and advocate of all things futurish, who phoned me in giddy delight the day he got the press release announcing the robot vacuum. "This is it, the future is finally coming," he said, almost hyperventilating. The personal jetpack, the dome colonies of Mars, and the T-bone dinner in a pill would be along shortly, he felt, along with all the other wonders *Popular Science* magazine had promised us when we were children. Dave died before he saw any of that and I will too, most likely. Both of us liked a drink too much to be trusted with a jetpack, anyway.

When we took Dave out of the box and set him up Bobo came over and gave an obligatory sniff. This wasn't simple, either—Bobo spent several minutes trying to figure out which end was which, and neither was really satisfactory, sniff-wise.

We programmed the vacuum to start up every morning at 9:00 a.m. and clean the main floor. Dave sat patiently in his docking station behind the elephant-ear plant overnight, charging his batteries, then beeped and whirred into life the next morning. Bobo was not prepared for this. He was used to us bringing strange things home and unboxing them, but once assembled they generally stayed put. This thing sat there feigning innocence then leapt out like a trapdoor spider lunging for prey.

It got worse. Dave has a real talent for knowing where Bobo is—if he's in the bedroom, Dave heads straight for him. If he's in my office, Dave is hot on his trail. I will be typing and Dave will bustle in, chasing Bobo.

There's no rest. Dave will give the room a once-over and be back out the door. I can hear Bobo growling again and the nervous skitter of toenails on the floor as he makes another strategic retreat. It's like the chase sequence in *Butch Cassidy and the Sundance Kid*—"Who are these guys?"—if Butch and Sundance were dogs and they were being pursued by a small black robot.

The point is, Dave is relentless and when Bobo has finally had enough and turns to fight, locking his legs and growling his to-the-death growl, Dave observes none of the dog protocol for such occasions. Civilized creatures have rituals for this sort of thing, facing off and threatening each other with bared teeth and loud threats of imminent dismemberment. Often, honour can be satisfied with this alone and both parties can retire with their dignity intact.

Not with Dave. Bobo turns and barks, stiff-legged, line drawn in the sand beyond which They Shall Not Pass, but Dave just keeps coming, beeping and whirring like some homicidal metal trilobite. Bobo can only screw up his courage and bolt past him, back legs threatening to overtake his front ones. Cornered, I've seen Bobo jump over the vacuum with a look of sheer desperation in his eyes.

To add insult to all this, Bobo is a notoriously sloppy eater and only about half the kibble in his mouth ever makes it to his stomach. The rest is scattered around his bowl, and Dave makes a great show of banging into the metal dish and loudly scooping up Bobo's leavings in a most insulting fashion while Bobo retreats to the foot of the bed in shame as his adversary literally eats his lunch.

Bobo has not had much luck with mechanical devices, large or small. Our house sits halfway up a small mountain and the summer we moved in, Bobo was exploring the road that passes our place and continues winding up the hill. He was just out of sight, last seen sniffing at the grass and weeds on the shoulder of the tarmac, when we heard a short honk from a car.

We looked up to see Bobo coming around the bend, in the middle of the road, heading down the hill with a pickup truck just behind him. He was trotting at a steady clip, a look of deep concern bordering on panic in his eyes. Down the hill they came in a low-speed chase, Bobo turning nervously every few steps to see if the thing was still following him and the driver hitting the horn every few seconds to encourage Bo to get out of the way.

By the time they got to our driveway Bobo was a nervous wreck and the exasperated driver wasn't doing much better. He tried to go around but Bobo has the same strange, sixth sense that little old ladies in supermarket aisles have, enabling them to stay right in front of you, anticipating and blocking your every move no matter how you try to get past them. I called him and Bobo ran for the driveway while the truck pulled away with the driver yelling something at us. Bobo stared after him and barked a few times for appearance's sake but his heart wasn't in it. He didn't care who won, he was just glad the whole exhausting business was over.

He looks like a ferocious Rottweiler but as I've said, just doesn't have the goods. He is, as one would describe a boy who can't climb trees and would rather make daisy-chains and press leaves in a book, delicate.

This is a dog who bites his nails. When we feed him scraps from the table he will balk at them unless they're offered on the end of the fork, so that he can take them in what can only be described as a dainty manner, or presented by hand after being torn into bite-size pieces, although he could easily bite through the kitchen chair I'm sitting on while I do it.

Our postman carries Milk-Bones in his satchel and everyday he throws two or three up onto the deck, where Bobo is generally standing and giving his customary bipolar welcome: growling and wagging his tail furiously. His dog DNA, genetically encoded to protect the home, suffers from a total failure to communicate with his *Yay! New friends!* nature. A Freudian would say that he suffers from a conflict between his Id and his Superego. Bobo would say, *Lie on the couch? I'm in.*

One day Bobo and I were getting into the car as the postman arrived and he handed the cookie directly to Bobo, who took it gently, wagged his tail, then walked away a few feet and spat it out, standing there with an expectant look on his face.

"He doesn't like them?" the postie asked me, confused. He'd been tossing them up onto the deck in good faith for months but never actually saw Bobo eat them. It seemed reasonable to assume he did, not knowing that they lay there until one of us gathered them up and made the necessary adjustments.

"He likes them fine but you have to break them in half," I said, and demonstrated. Once it was snapped in two Bobo ate both pieces in short order and indicated he wouldn't mind a few more. The postie was confused by this and I told him that was all right, I was, too. We left it at that.

My only answer is simply that Bobo is by nature an exceedingly gentle person. He doesn't like loud noises, unless he's the one making them, and at any sign of violence he runs and jumps on the bed. Even a serious argument will send him to the other end of the house.

When it rains and I let him out, he stands under the roof overhang to do his business and won't even do that until he's gone around the house to make sure it's really raining on all four sides of the property. He'll walk a considerable distance out of his way to avoid the gravel path because it hurts his feet and when he does have to cross gravel, like a parking lot, he does it high-stepping like a Lipizzaner stallion.

He's 150 pounds of muscles and teeth with the disposition of a hamster. In fact, the one time he met a hamster he licked it—not an exploratory slurp to see what it tasted like, but the way a mother licks her puppies. The hamster didn't much care for it and I was more afraid that he would bite Bobo than the other way round.

When I take him to feed the ducks at the park, he chases them and they just sit there, treading water, which makes it a very short exercise. Bo stops at the edge of the pond and stares at them and they look back with a dismissive, wholly unconcerned attitude that is, frankly, insulting.

This is a dog who has to wear a bright orange life jacket when we go to the lake in the summer, because he is so anxious and determined to stay right beside us he'll come out to where Penny and I are floating on an air mattress and swim circles around us looking for a way up onto it until he can't go another stroke and starts to slip under the water. The one and only time that happened I held him up by his collar and paddled like hell with my other hand until we got him back to shore. Now he wears the vest, which is surely the dog equivalent of orthopedic shoes, and if the rest of the Rottweilers ever see how stupid he looks in it, they'll take away his union card.

Rip was equally loyal and loving but he enjoyed a good fight, even the ones he lost. He backed down from nothing and no one. Once he got loose from the backyard and wandered out front into the street where he was knocked down by a car. It was a gentle knockdown, the driver saw him and hit the brakes and wasn't going that fast to begin with, but Rip took the mandatory count and I came around the side of the building just in time to see him get up, wobble a few feet as he collected his wits, then turn and advance, hackles up, snarling and biting at the front grill of the car that hit him. He was ready to do battle with a midsize import and it was all I could do to pull him away.

Bobo, by way of comparison, will go walkabout while I'm digging in the garden or occupied with some chore and the next thing I know there's a horn blowing and Bobo is halfway up the hill, in the middle of the road, blocking a car. If the horn doesn't scare him—if he happened to be looking that way and saw the car first—he considers it a friendly hello and wanders up to the driver's side looking for a pat and a neck scratch. This is generally enough to frighten most drivers. I imagine it's a bit like having the biggest guy in a rough bar get up from his beer and walk towards your table without saying a word, staring straight at you all the while. By the time Bobo gets to the side of the car they've generally discovered urgent business elsewhere and cleared out when all they needed to do was roll the window down and rub his ear. Then again, if he weren't my dog, I wouldn't do it either.

We have squirrels and rabbits in the yard all year, and although they do keep an eye on Bobo, it couldn't properly be described as anything like fear. It's more like, *Oh—him again.* The rabbits continue nibbling grass until Bobo makes his move and then hop nonchalantly into the woods. He sniffs and paces around for a bit, convinced he's got them cornered, but we can see the rabbit through the underbrush, chewing calmly. Satisfied he's shown the flag and put things right in his kingdom Bobo trots back towards us with real pride while the rabbit shuffles back out to grab another choice mouthful. The squirrels are worse, running him through the brush until they finally bolt up a tree trunk and then sit on a low branch sneering at him and laughing. But the final insult is a chipmunk who lives in the giant dogwood out back who makes a squeaking sound exactly like one of Bobo's chew toys.

Bobo will stand underneath it for hours trying to figure out how his rubber bone got up there.

And it doesn't end outside. Oh no, the abuse continues inside the house. Penny and I had agreed, probably after a few days of babysitting Seamus, that one dog in the house was sufficient to requirements. As noted, Seamus is more of a traditionalist than Bobo and because our property can't really be fenced that means both he and Bobo spend a good deal of time inside the house or out on the large wraparound deck overlooking the valley. To Seamus's mind, this is not so much a relaxation area as a forward command post and gymnasium. It has long been established that whatever a dog can see, hear, or smell from a window or porch constitutes the natural boundaries of His Yard.

Consequently, Bobo and Seamus keep a vigilant watch from the deck in order to protect us from package delivery, the constant threat of elderly walkers taking their constitutional, children of all sizes going up and down the hill, the school bus, and certain cars—some require extensive barking, others not, based on some dog criteria we've never been able to figure out.

When the world is safe again, it's time to relax with some racing and wrestling. Work hard, play hard—that's Seamus's motto. He runs at top speed from one end of the deck to the other, makes a 180-degree turn a Kentucky bootlegger would envy and roars back the way he came, tongue flapping, ears streaming and Bobo bouncing and barking in encouragement.

After he's sufficiently warmed up Seamus likes to play-fight, and while slow off the mark in other areas, Bobo has become a big fan of this sport. They roll and tumble over each other, snapping and growling, spit flying, patio furniture crashing in their wake, regularly bouncing off the sliding glass doors and the metal railings, until someone opens the door and yells at them. Then they stand there, eyes bugged out, panting, chests heaving, trailing snot and saliva, and looking thoroughly mad.

People have said having dogs in the house is like having children who are stuck at the age of two permanently. In our case, it's like having two hyperactive Sumo wrestlers and as I said, we've long ago agreed that one is more than plenty.

Or at least I thought we'd agreed. One day Penny answered the phone and from what I could hear from my office, based on the squeals and shrieks, either we'd won the lottery or some previously unknown, wealthy relative had died.

It was my sister-in-law, a hairdresser, calling to say that a client of hers had two black pugs she needed to find a home for. In most instances this would be met by "Well, good luck with that," or even "Hey, do I call you up with my problems?" But it needs to be understood that the MacNeils and Daltons, which clan I have been adopted into, suffer from Pug Envy.

Growing up Penny had a black pug named Uggy which she dressed up and pushed around the neigh-

174

bourhood in a stroller. (She also had a cat named Potter which spent a good deal of his time stuffed into a tube sock and carted about. He is alleged to have enjoyed it but I have my doubts.) The sister-in-law, Paddy, and her husband Arleigh have two pugs of their own, Charlie and Sally, and my mother-in-law Susan sews Hallowe'en costumes for them. Both the kids are similarly pug-happy, as is my father-in-law, who pretends otherwise and fools no one. It's something that can't be explained any more than people who enjoy making balls out of tinfoil or jogging. Some people are apparently born with a predisposition to these things, like alcoholics.

In this case, I married into a family who are clearly powerless over pugs. These are people who have pug plates—"Look what I found at the Antiques Mall!"—and pug salt and pepper shakers.

I was undone by a technicality; while we had agreed that one dog was enough, pugs are demonstrably not any kind of real dog. What they are is unclear—Arleigh says they're "potatoes with a heartbeat" and when I look at one all I see is a pork roast covered in hair. They look like what you would feed to a real dog, like the tiny aquarium fish bred as food.

The encyclopedia says they came from China, originally bred as lap dogs for the royal classes and called Lo-Sze or "Foos" and were used as the models for the ornamental dragons that fill Chinatown souvenir shops and are traditionally placed outside homes and temples as guardians.

They're also called "lion dogs," due, I would think, to their complete and perfect ignorance of what they actually are. No pug has apparently ever looked into a mirror, or if they did, they are capable of an unmatched level of self-delusion. They're fearless, I'll give them that if nothing else. But I think it's telling that the first Emperor of China, Qin Shi Huang, destroyed by royal decree every written record and work of art related to the pug at some point between 221 and 210 BCE.

It was a nice try but Shi Huang failed to stop the pug's relentless march out of China (actually they were carried out by Tibetan monks, because their under-sized legs make them ill-suited for marching, or much else) and from there through Japan and into Europe, after which they were free to run rampant throughout the world. By which I mean carried, or possibly on a series of short walks on the leash as they defy training, obey no one, and, as noted, can't go far on those stubby legs.

My own theory is that they came from space. All the evidence supports it. They are physically ill-equipped to survive on this planet: they cannot hunt or find food for themselves and must be fed a careful diet. They must be constantly monitored for a multitude of dis-eases and chronic conditions, many of them respira-tory in nature — just the sort of thing one would expect from a creature not originally designed to breathe our atmosphere. And the constant snuffling, muttering, and chirping is nothing more than conversation in their own language.

176

Despite what I consider conclusive evidence of this invasion it makes no difference at this late date. The war was lost centuries ago and we are only tolerated because the conquerors need someone to lift them on and off things. Whether their inability to do so themselves is a result of Earth's higher gravity or those ridiculous, stumpy little legs is moot at this point.

And what does Bobo think about this? Not a lot. At best he's . . . intrigued and a little confused. His only experience with other dogs in the house is Seamus, and for the first day or two of his visits he's happy to have Seamus here. There's some novelty to it and some entertainment value. But both Bobo and I agree with Ben Franklin; after three days, fish, house-guests and other people's dogs should be tossed out. By the end of a week Bobo doesn't even go to the door when Penny's ex comes to collect Seamus. At that point he believes Seamus's most attractive side is his backside, walking away.

But at least Seamus does eventually leave. The pugs just showed up one day with a worrying amount of luggage—wire crates and kennels, dishes, leashes, eye drops, a large box full of other medications and toiletries and special food that Bobo isn't allowed to eat. It would be the equivalent for you and I of some rattletrap pickup truck rolling into the yard with your hillbilly relatives and all their worldly possessions, obviously intent on an open-ended stay. *Howdy, cuz!*

They're loud, they're everywhere and their ways are not ours. They have no sense of decorum or, frankly, manners of any kind. Bobo has to watch as their meals are scooped out from the Special Bag of Forbidden Food and when they've vacuumed it up, in short order—they feed like piranha—they try to shove in beside Bobo at his dish. Failing that they'll stand behind him and stare when he eats, waiting for stray bits of kibble and a friendly bounce, and this makes him very nervous.

As I say, somehow pugs have been able to maintain an impressive ignorance of who and what they actually are. In their minds, and in their behaviour, they truly believe they're fearsome beasts and when Bobo growls at them to back off, they're not having any of it. They growl back and bark and snap, or come as close to snapping as something without an actual snout can.

Between the pugs and Dave the vacuum cleaner Bobo feels more than a little ganged-up on. I can't say I blame him, either. When Bobo backs away and I rescue his food dish, they surround him and nip at his ankles, front and back. When he runs away they give chase and harry him around the house, yapping and barking while Bobo skitters on the laminate floor trying to get some distance between him and them, enough so he can think for a minute and figure out how it all went so terribly wrong.

Of course, he could settle their miniscule hash with a maximum of two good bites but he won't do it, and they know it. It's a bit like the professional boxer being harassed by a drunk at some nightclub; he can't hit him, even to protect himself, and in Bobo's case he can't even pay his tab and leave.

When they're on the attack they remind me of a movie I saw when I was a teenager, about a woman who somehow ends up in possession of a small voodoo doll, complete with warpaint, bone through its nose, grass skirt, and spear. That night the doll comes to life and hunts her through the apartment, climbing up the draperies to jump at her, darting out from under the furniture to stab her feet and generally making life miserable. I think she finally throws him into the oven and broils him, and both Bobo and I quietly agree that there's nothing wrong with pugs that a few hours at about 425 degrees wouldn't fix.

Actually, the easiest remedy would be to look the other way when loading the dishwasher. I need one hand to put the dishes in and one to pull pugs back as they try to crawl in and lick the dirty plates; just wait until a night when the plates are nicely covered in gravy or cheese sauce, leave the door open and unattended then come back and set the damn thing on Sanitize.

When they're not attacking they ignore him. They refuse to move out of the way and Bobo has to skirt around them, growling softly. If he's between them and someplace they want to be, they simply walk under him, which Bobo finds more than a little disconcerting. They also seem to be exempt from all the laws regarding what dogs are and aren't allowed to do, such as sleeping on the couch or the bed. I have learned not to question this though.

For my part, this is not how I saw my declining years, either, standing half-asleep in wet grass at two a.m. crooning "good girl" to a snuffling, chattering lump that refuses to urinate. They have to be leashed when outside, because pugs follow the wind with no regard for commands, threats, or, for that matter, begging. They go where they will, and at good speed, considering their design flaws. As much as the thought of pugs disappearing over the hill, never to be seen again, has its attraction, in the long-term it's not a solution Penny would buy. Nor would she believe they were "carried away by eagles," which has crossed my mind a few times.

No, Bobo and I are stuck with them for anywhere from twelve to fourteen years and the way they're coddled and fussed over, they may simply refuse to die at all.

People ask, "What is love?" I'll tell you: love is standing in a parking lot holding the leashes for two pugs that are grunting and snuffling the ground like truffle-hunting hogs while your wife is inside the pet store buying Pug Chow. It plays hell with a man's self-image. The frightening thing is I'm afraid I'm becoming fond of them despite myself.

*Chapter Fourteen*

# A Series of Dogs

*If there are no dogs in Heaven, then when I die I
want to go where they went.*

— WILL ROGERS

The poet wrote, "I have measured out my life with
coffee spoons," which is one way of doing it, but I prefer to lay mine out as a series of dogs, all of them in an
unlikely line from the very first to the latest, and when
someone says "dog years" I think of how many dogs I
may have left in me.

I know they're talking about the formula for figuring your dog's age in human years, with one of theirs
equivalent to seven of ours. It's a shorthand measure of
longevity, but I doubt both its accuracy and its scope.
I've always thought it was better used as a comparison
of value: to a dog properly loved and appreciated his
year is seven times as enjoyable and fulfilling as any
one of ours.

But there are years and then there are years, and it
should be noted that dogs do not reckon time as we

do. This needs to be factored into any consideration of "dog time" and "dog years." Scientists say dogs have no actual sense of time as we do, with the past back there and the future up ahead, like a freight train hauling months and minutes and a grim black caboose at the end. They live in an eternal now and they suffer for it; whether you're gone five minutes or five years, they only know you were here once and now you're gone, possibly forever.

Dogs are either/or creatures and time is like a light switch, on or off, good or bad. When he was away, Robert E. Lee wrote letters home to his horse, Traveller, and in one said, "Tell him I miss him dreadfully and repented of our separation but once, and that is the whole time since we parted." Which is about how your dog feels when you go away. Strangely, no one has ever explored how long a year feels to a human who is used to being with a dog and suddenly finds themselves without one. I can tell them the answer: an eternity. Hell must be a place with no dogs.

When it's bad for dogs it's endlessly bad, but they can bounce back in a way we never could. If you or I could go from despondency to ecstatic joy as fast as our dogs, they'd be delivering our lithium in a dump truck.

My last three dogs have been Rottweilers and for all their virtues they are tragically short-lived, averaging about ten years or less. Dog people call the big dogs "heartbreak breeds" for just that reason. This week Bobo tried to jump up on the bed beside me and couldn't make it. I've had to cut a large piece of foam to lay under his blanket and pillow because the floor is getting too hard for him and he's started to cry sometimes when he gets up in the morning. Some nights I have to get up and make a peanut butter-and-aspirin sandwich for him.

I've been here before and I dread the process, which has already begun. My own line doesn't tend to long life either, with most of us dead before seventy, and I also spent my first forty years flipping a middle finger at the Reaper and calling him rude names, which didn't help my prospects either. Not that it matters—in the end, he always wins. You can argue sports, you can argue politics, you can even argue religion, but you can't argue with genetics and the actuarial tables. Better to take a page from your dog's book and fill the days you have left rather than pine there aren't more of them.

By conservative estimate I should have at least two more Rottweilers in me, and when I do run out of dogs and time I hope they bury me in a park, under an inviting tree, and that the lack of a God does not preclude the possibility of a heaven, and that when I get there, all the dogs of my life run to meet me, carrying my lost socks in their mouths.

That doesn't seem like too much to ask.